DOING TIME
A Look at Crime and Prisons

DOING TIME

A Look at Crime and Prisons

by
PHYLLIS ELPERIN CLARK and
ROBERT LEHRMAN

Illustrated with prints and photographs

HASTINGS HOUSE · PUBLISHERS

NEW YORK

365
c

To our parents:
William J. and Natalie R. Elperin,
and Harry and Beatrice Lehrman

Library of Congress Cataloging in Publication Data

Clark, Phyllis Elperin   Doing time.

  Bibliography
  Includes index.
  1. Prisons—United States. 2. Criminal justice,
Administration of—United States. I. Lehrman, Robert A.
joint author. II. Title.
HV9471.C55   1980   365'.973   80-178
ISBN 0-8038-1566-2

Published simultaneously in Canada by Saunders of
Toronto, Ltd., Don Mills, Ontario

Designed by Al Lichtenberg
Printed in the United States of America

Contents

Acknowledgements   6

1 What Am I Doing Here?   9
2 In the Beginning   19
3 The Reformers   35
4 "The Prisoner Has the Advantage"   46
5 The New Sciences   56
6 How Do They Get There?   67
7 Inside   87
8 Getting Out   109
9 What's Next?   123
10 A Last Word   140

Bibliography   148
Index   151

Acknowledgements

To write *Doing Time* was to walk a succession of tightropes. There was the tightrope between readability and accuracy. There was the tightrope between frankness and sensationalism. There was the tightrope between making judgements and slanting material.

We owe a lot to Judy Donnelly, our editor, for helping us walk those tightropes in relative safety. We want to thank Elise Berkower and Elizabeth Catenaccio for their help with research and in finding illustrations. Thanks also to Steve Schoen and Maggie Sherwood of the Floating Foundation of Photography who supplied us with sensitive and striking photos taken by inmates of New York State prisons.

We owe a large debt to many people associated with the Dwight Correctional Center. We are especially indebted to Herbert E. Bailey, former Assistant Warden of Operations, who guided us to areas of great interest and then cleared obstacles, allowing us access to inmates. Warden Robert Buchanan was most willing to open the prison doors on our subsequent visits. Gary Curl, Jane Higgins Huch and Carol Kelly of the Work Release Staff; Kay Hayes Buchanan and Lois Guyon, social workers; Sue Welch, psychologist; and James Ritter, teacher, gave us valuable insights into prison life and conditions. And we are deeply grateful to the 100 Dwight inmates who were frank, cooperative and generous with their time and energy.

We would also like to thank the inmates and the staff of Green Haven State Prison for their patience and cooperation.

We are deeply grateful, too, for the assistance provided by many employees of the Illinois Department of Corrections, the Illinois Law Enforcement Commission, the staff and residents of the Peoria Community Correctional Center, the Morton Grove Police Department, the Law Enforcement Assistance Association, United States Department of Justice, the John Howard Association, the Chicago Crime Commission, the New York State Division of Criminal Justice Services, Donald K. Woolley, and University of Iowa Professors John R Winnie, John Schulze and the late Malcolm S. MacLean, Jr.

As interpreters of a complex and controversial subject, we owe a debt to the many people who have spent their lives writing and researching in criminology and penology.

In a special way, we are grateful to Sean Aaron Clark for being a pleasant, cooperative little companion on the road, in libraries, in law enforcement agencies and at home.

Finally, we wish to thank our spouses, Mark Clark and Susan Thaul, for their understanding and tolerance.

Dwight Correctional Center; Illinois.

1

What Am I Doing Here?

One day, a few years back, a police car drove through the gates of a series of big brick buildings that make up the Correctional Center in Dwight, Illinois. The police were coming to drop off a 20-year-old girl named Tina Wright—blond, freckle faced, and a convicted felon.

Since her fifteenth birthday, Tina had been arrested three times. She had spent a few months in a juvenile home. But this was the first time she had ever been inside a prison, and, as she got out of the car, she found it a little hard to believe that the high brick walls studded with iron hooks were meant for her.

Inside, she was stripped, searched, given the grey dress all inmates had to wear, and shown to her cell.

Tina looked out through the bars in her little window. Three days before at this time she might have been shopping, or else having lunch with some friends. And at that moment it began to sink in that for the next three years her life would be very different. She remembers thinking, "What am I doing here?"

Most Americans would simply answer: "She committed a

9

crime and she has to pay for it." After all, earlier in the year, Tina and three of her friends had gotten a gun and held up a gas station; they forced the gas station attendant to open his safe, took the money, then locked him in a back room and drove off.

The gas station attendant had recognized one of Tina's friends. Within a few days the police had arrested all four, and when her lawyer told her that pleading guilty would result in a lighter sentence, Tina confessed. The judge sentenced her to three years at Dwight.

"She's got to be punished," one of the prison staff members said. "Maybe in prison she'll learn to obey the law."

And so Tina joined over 200,000 other men and women who that year were serving sentences—"doing time" in American prisons.

Prisons have become an enormously controversial topic. There are criminologists who argue that prisons are useless and that the whole system should be dismantled. Others, supported by many public figures, argue that we need more prisons and stiffer sentences. Some say we are too tough on criminals. Some say we are not tough enough. The debate raises some basic questions about crime and criminals.

What is a crime? It is not simply "doing something wrong." To most criminologists, a crime must have several characteristics. The act must cause harm and be legally forbidden: there must be a law against it. It must be intentional. And the law must set some punishment for it.

Tina, for example, committed an armed robbery, which is clearly forbidden under the laws of her state. She meant to do it; it involved loss of money and threat to life and thus was harmful. And the law proposes a prison sentence as punishment. So, Tina was sent to prison.

Prisons are not to be confused with jails. The nearly 4,000 jails in cities, towns, and counties throughout the United States are used to hold people accused of breaking the law until they can have a trial, as well as to house those convicted

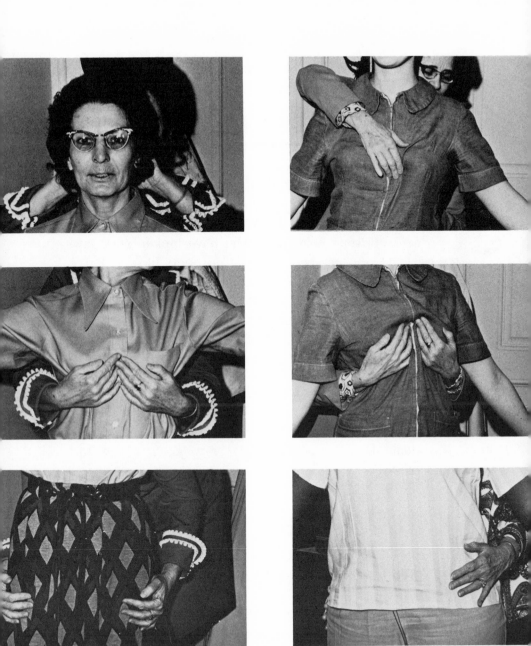

The Frisk. Dwight Correctional Center; Illinois.

of certain minor offenses such as public drunkenness. Prisons are institutions used to hold convicted criminals while they serve their sentences.

There are two types. *Federal* prisons hold people who have broken laws made by the Congress of the United States. The inmates have, for example, kidnapped children, sold military secrets to other governments, taken stolen material across state lines, or committed crimes in more than one state. There were about 26,000 such federal inmates in 1979.

State prisons hold those who have broken state laws. In most state prisons about half the prisoners have stolen something; in 1979 roughly 260,000 people were held in about 400 state prison facilities in America.

Why are people in prison? Percentages differ a little from year to year. Still, this table of crime statistics, based on convicted criminals serving time in state prisons* provides one answer.

Crime	Percent of convicted state criminals
Robbery	22.5
Homicide	18.1
Burglary	18.0
Drug Crimes	10.0
Larceny	6.5
Sex Crimes (including rape)	6.3
All Others (including forgery, embezzlement, fraud, theft, assault, auto theft)	18.0

But, in a larger sense, these lawbreakers are in prison for other reasons—many of them because of social and environmental factors only dimly understood even by experts.

"You will not eliminate crime by eliminating poverty, ignorance, poor health and ugly environments," wrote former U.S. Attorney General Ramsey Clark, "but it is clear that such conditions are demonstrably responsible for most crime."

*Based on L.E.A.A. figures as cited in "Who Is in Prison," by James Q. Wilson, *Commentary,* November, 1976.

It is true that crime flourishes in our poorest communities. But it is also true that most poor people do not commit major crimes. Criminologists, therefore, have sought the roots of crime in other areas. What is the relationship, they ask, between crime and personality? The home and family? Religion? Schools? Race? How, they ask, does the emphasis on individual success in American culture affect the crime rate?

There is much they do not know. The causes of crime are complex. It is important to bear this in mind. And as the causes are complex, so is the prevention.

In talking about Tina earlier, the Dwight staff member used the word "punish." Defined by one dictionary as "to afflict with pain, loss or suffering for a crime or fault"; it is a crucial word. At the heart of our prison system lies the belief that those who break the law should be punished. And people who believe that usually give two reasons:

Retribution. It is not unusual to want revenge when we have been hurt—to feel a need to strike back. In this same way, society wants to get back at the lawbreaker. We have all seen episodes in TV westerns where an angry mob tries to lynch a prisoner. When the sheriff holds off the crowd by saying, "He'll get what's coming to him—after the trial," he is acknowledging that he wants revenge, too. The trial is his formal, socially approved means of achieving it.

Some philosophers and politicians argue that we should resist the impulse for revenge—that we should use reason, not emotion, in deciding how to handle criminals. Others emphasize that retribution is healthy. It is like shouting when one is angry. One state senator, defending the death penalty said, "This is simply the natural response of society to a heinous crime."

Deterrence. Most defenders of the prison system argue that punishment "deters," or prevents crime. Students know they will be punished if caught cheating on an exam; therefore, they keep their eyes on their own papers. There are those who believe that punishing the burglar or murderer brings similar results.

Thus, in eighteenth-century England, great crowds were allowed to gather at public hangings, on the theory that they would be so horrified they would remain law-abiding citizens.

A modern city attorney explained the deterrence theory by remembering his own childhood: "I had been misbehaving," he said, "and my father gave me an awful whaling and he had to do it only once. It is the same way with criminals. You must inflict pain to get results."

Retribution and deterrence may provide justification for punishing the criminal. But throughout history there have been many ways to inflict punishment. Why send the law-breaker to prison?

Defenders of the prison system offer two arguments:

Incapacitation. Someone serving a prison term can't harm society. Tina might want to rob another gas station. But if she is locked in her cell she can't put that plan into action.

Secondly, and most important: *rehabilitation.*

Rehabilitation, to penologists, means using prison as a means to change the criminal so he or she will no longer want to commit crimes.

Today, most prisons are much more than cellblocks; they try to prepare inmates to return to society. At Dwight, for example, Tina was taught some skills in the hope that when she left she might be able to find work. She met with a counselor once a week to discuss her problems. She was urged to take courses at the prison school.

The problem, though, is that more and more penologists doubt that prisons either deter or rehabilitate. They feel the evidence may even point the other way.

In 1963, for example, the Supreme Court said that all poor defendants had a right to a lawyer; as a result, the state of Florida had to release 1,252 prisoners who had been convicted without lawyers. They were set free long before their sentences

Sing Sing; New York.

were finished. The Florida Department of Corrections later
compared these prisoners with a similar group who had served
their sentences in full. The result: 25% of the prisoners who
had served the full term had committed crimes again. But only
13.6% of the prisoners who had been released early had
done so.

Critics of American prisons point to such a study and ask:
is it possible that long-term prison confinement actually en-
courages people to commit more crimes?

Prison life, despite the refinements of the twentieth century, is, for the most part, brutal.

"I think," said one South Carolina judge in the 1950's
after a tour of South Carolina's Central Correctional Institution, "the state should take a bulldozer and push that penitentiary into the sewer. I've sent my last man to that prison. There
are cells in there 3½ feet wide and 8 feet long."

And today, some Texas prisons crowd three inmates into 5 x 9 foot cells, forcing one to sleep on the floor. In South Carolina, 8000 inmates are crammed into prisons designed for 4600. Even the 'best' prisons are dehumanizing. They are noisy, crowded, and regimented. Above all, they are violent.

"The ball and chain and the rock pile are gone," writes Charles Silberman in his 1979 book, *Criminal Violence, Criminal Justice,* "Yet prisons, especially the maximum security institutions which contain the majority of the inmate population, remain brutal and brutalizing places. In the last few years, federal courts have held that living conditions in prisons in Alabama, Arkansas, Florida, Louisiana, Mississippi and Rhode Island have violated the Eighth Amendment's prohibition against 'cruel and unusual punishment.' " How can subjecting people to such conditions, critics ask, fail to make them bitter and resentful of society?

United States Supreme Court Chief Justice Warren Burger put it this way: "To cast the guilty into nineteenth century penal institutions" is "folly . . . It is wrong. It is expensive. It is stupid."

It has become commonplace to call prisons "schools" for crime. For, after all, how can you persuade lawbreakers to change when you surround them with cellmates and buddies who have robbed, murdered, or assaulted people? One repeater put it this way: "When I was in the joint," he said, "cons taught me tricks I'd never thought of."

Finally, the critics of our prison system feel that prisons, and every other element in our criminal justice system, discriminate against the poor and against minorities. Nonwhites make up about 12.5% of the population of the United States but almost half of our prison population. To some, this means simply that black people must be chronic lawbreakers.

A few years back, a sociology class in one California school wanted to test whether police showed prejudice. A dozen students—black and white—were selected. All had perfect driving records. At the time, one of the most controversial groups in

Sing Sing; New York.

California was the militant Black Panther Party. So these students were asked to drive to school and back each day with Black Panther bumper stickers on their cars.

In less than three weeks, they had 30 tickets. Two students had to stop driving because their licenses were suspended. Soon the experiment had to be dropped because the $1,000 the class had budgeted was used up on fines and court costs.

The relationship of race and crime in America is a complex and sensitive subject. How many blacks and other minorities are imprisoned for crimes while whites who have committed the same offenses are let off? The data is unclear. But certainly racism is a factor in the disposal of cases involving black suspects. It is a major factor in the day-to-day lives of most inmates. How, the critics ask, does this square with American ideas of justice?

These are serious questions. Yet the possibility that

prisons don't work is one that many of us find hard to swallow. "Look at the billions of dollars we spend!" we say. "Look at the buildings! Look at the hundreds of thousands of men and women—police, guards, judges—working within the criminal justice system! Somebody must know what he's doing!"

Yet the literature of prison reform is filled with pessimism.

"By what criteria," asks David Rothman, in his influential book, *The Discovery of the Asylum,* "is a penitentiary an improvement over the stocks or a system of fines and whippings?"

"Prisons have few friends," writes Norval Morris, a New Zealander who has become one of the most important writers on prison reform in America, "dissatisfaction is widespread."

"Prisons are intrinsically evil," writes Jessica Mitford in her best-seller, *Kind and Usual Punishment,* "and should be abolished."

In a few chapters we will look closely at prison life today—for Tina and for other inmates. But first we should ask how the idea of prison took root in our culture. It is surprising to learn that for most of Western history, the prison sentence was practically unknown.

⊂ᵇ *2*

In the Beginning

About 3,500 years ago a woman named Ayinlungu living in what is now Iran accused a man of having promised her a gift but failing to deliver. The man denied it.

We would hardly consider this a criminal matter. But in Elam—an ancient civilization with its own criminal and civil code—the woman could take the matter to court. And she did.

She came with ten witnesses. The judge, though, had his own idea about what constituted proof. He ordered Ayinlungu to "submit to divine judgment." This meant she would be thrown in the river; if she sank, she lost her case. Otherwise, the man would have to make good his promise.

We are lucky enough to know all this because over the last century archeologists have worked painstakingly to excavate the cities of Elam. They have deciphered hundreds of bricks inscribed with case histories from Elamite courts. These records provide some of the earliest documented accounts of crime and punishment anywhere in human history.

There is no mention of prison. Punishments involved mutilation or death—or loss of protection from the gods. A per-

Expressions like "throw them to the dogs" actually referred to one ancient form of capital punishment.

jurer—one who lies before a court—for example, would have his "hand and tongue cut off." He had to pay a fine and had to forfeit protection of the god Inshushinak "thus losing his peace and his life at a blow."

How did early people draw up their criminal codes? How did they decide innocence or guilt? How did they punish the guilty?

In the case of the Elamites we have written records to guide us. When it comes to prehistoric men and women the answers are murkier. It would be convenient if all regions of the world developed the same legal codes at the same time and wrote them down in English. In fact, regions differ and our theories include a lot of educated guesswork.

Generally speaking, though, historians believe that primitive tribal societies looked to religion to answer many of their questions about the world around them. They believed that the forces of nature were directly controlled by the gods, and naturally, they did their best to keep the gods happy. If a flood, an earthquake, or an epidemic troubled their village, they suspected that someone in their group had broken one of the gods' laws. A person whose actions angered the gods put the whole tribe in danger, and his punishment could be serious: the culprit might be killed or driven into the wilderness, where he would almost certainly die of hunger.

Surprisingly, the crimes that seem most serious to us today, like theft, rape, and murder, were often treated as family matters and dealt with privately. If a man were murdered, it was up to his family, or clan, to get revenge. The rest of the tribe did not interfere. Since tribes were usually quite small, it was possible to deal with offenses on a personal level. Very few crimes were committed by strangers. And very few people were able to commit the same crime over and over again; the risks of being caught by one's neighbors were great.

Revenge sometimes got out of hand. The family of a man who was killed in revenge for a murder might not agree that their kinsman had deserved to die. They, in turn, would try to avenge his death. Quarrels between two families sometimes led to a "blood feud" that could spread to the distant relatives of the original parties. Such a feud might not end until all the men in both families had been killed off. The whole tribe might be seriously weakened as a result.

As populations grew larger, private justice did not work very well. For example, quarrels were more likely to arise between strangers, and enforcing the system became difficult. Gradually, in Babylonia, Persia, and Rome, crime became the concern of the community. The ruler decided what was legal and what was not, and he or his appointed judges set the penalties.

In addition, communities began to add to the list of illegal acts—a citizen of the military state of Sparta, for example, could be whipped for being too fat. Also, the chief motive for punishing criminals was no longer to satisfy the victims or their families, but to set an example for everyone. Punishments were usually swift and severe. The Sumerian law codes of Lipit Ishtar and Eshunna, which date from about 1800 B.C. in the same region as Elam, set up a system of punishments based on mutilation: a counterfeiter might have his hand cut off. Whipping was also common. In fact, this punishment is described in detail in the Bible: judges in the book of Deuteronomy had the power to order the guilty party whipped on the spot and to decide how many lashes the offender would receive. "According to the measure of the sin shall the measure also of the stripes be."

Criminals were often executed in those days, and the manner of death was usually painful and public. A lawbreaker might be stabbed to death or buried alive, and many ancient civilizations—the Chinese, the Assyrians, and the Romans among them—used crucifixion. Draco, a king in Greece about 700 B.C., imposed the death penalty for almost *every* crime. We still use the term "Draconian" to describe an especially harsh law.

What about prisons?

Flogging was a common punishment in ancient Egypt.

By and large, imprisonment was not used as punishment. In Roman times, criminals were sometimes sentenced to work in mines or at other especially dangerous and difficult jobs. Usually, though, lawbreakers were held in prisons only until their punishment could be carried out. Most people agreed with Ulpian, the third century Roman jurist who wrote: "A prison ought to be maintained for holding men, not for punishing them."

This view of prisons was shared by the Germanic tribes of the north. To avoid blood feuds, they developed a system called the *wer-geld,* which means "man-money." Every man, and every part of his body, was declared to have a certain value in money. Instead of demanding an eye for an eye, or a life for a life, victims and their families were expected to settle for the appropriate compensation. In one region, if a man's nose were cut, the criminal paid him a set amount. If it were lopped off completely, he received more. If a criminal could not pay his fine, he might be maimed, sold into slavery, or killed. The system seems to have worked. It lasted for many centuries, and when two of the Germanic tribes, the Angles and the Saxons, settled in England, they brought the notion of *wer-geld* with them. They used prisons mainly as a place to lock people up until they paid their *wer-geld* or fines.

When the Normans conquered England in 1066, two different systems of justice met. The Norman kings were not used to the Anglo-Saxon idea of leaving justice in private hands, but they were quick to see the advantage of fines as a form of punishment. They made one change, however: instead of paying the fines to their victims, offenders were now ordered to pay the money to the king.

Since the king now benefited from the fines, it became his responsibility to collect them. In 1154, King Henry II ordered *gaols* (pronounced jails) built in every county of England. The gaols were used to hold accused criminals until one of the king's judges could arrive to conduct a trial.

Picture those early English gaols: they were usually large, crowded rooms where men, women, and children slept together. In many prisons the rich and poor were separated. The rich could bring in servants, their own furniture, and even cooks who prepared special meals while the poor slept on straw or on the cold floor.

"It became customary," writes one student of English prisons, "for a gaol to be divided into . . . 'the common side' where the penniless prisoners eked out their days in squalor . . . and 'the master's side' where prisoners might obtain a graduated scale of comfort according to the amount of the rents they were paying."

The gaoler sometimes paid to be appointed to his post. Sometimes his appointment was a political reward. He had no salary, so he made as much money as he could from the prisoners. Prisoners had to pay the gaoler for food. They paid him for bedding—usually some moldy straw. If they wanted a fire, there was a fee for that. Even if a prisoner were pardoned or acquitted—even if the arrest had been a *mistake*—he had to pay a release fee before he could leave.

Prisoners died at five times the rate of free men and women. People believed that somehow the prisons themselves caused disease; actually rats and fleas caused the typhoid which was known as "gaol fever." There were no infirmaries, no medicines. Prisoners—sick or well—were only allowed outside the prison under guard to be in the streets. There were fights among the prisoners, drunkenness, and sex. There were no baths, so visitors often brought bouquets of flowers to mask the odor of the people they were visiting.

Rich or poor, prisoners stayed in the gaol only until a traveling judge came to town to hand down his verdicts. Then the punishment decided by the judge would take effect. This might be a fine, or it might be whipping, mutilation, or even hanging. Only in a few unusual cases did judges ever use gaol as a punishment in itself. In 1285, for example, one judge decreed that a lawyer who deceived the court should be sent to gaol for one year. And in 1361, the English adopted a law that called for anyone who stole a hawk to be sentenced to two years in the county gaol.

From our point of view, there is a great difference between ordering a thief to pay a fine and cutting off his hand. But these early forms of punishment had one thing in common. No one expected them to reform the criminal; as long as he did not get into trouble again, the law did not care about his motives or whether he was sorry for what he had done.

One group that did care very much about reforming wrongdoers, however, was the Church. The old connection between law and religion had not died out with the growth of community legal codes and the coming of Christianity. During the Middle Ages, the Church actually developed its own separate court system, and by the twelfth century any churchman accused of a crime, no matter what kind, had the right to be tried in a bishop's court. This privilege was called "benefit of clergy," and it was highly valued because the church courts were known to be much more lenient than ordinary civil courts.

Today only a tiny percentage of accused criminals are priests, ministers, or nuns, or have any connection to church authority. But in the Middle Ages, almost every educated person had studied in some form of church school, and an individ-

Medieval punishments were harsh, varied and frequent. Burning, beheading, drawing-and-quartering are among the few shown here.

ual's ability to read and write was taken as evidence that he or she came under the authority of the church. Strangely enough, the courts always used the same passage from the Bible as a reading test—a passage from the fifth Psalm that begins, "Have mercy upon me, O God, according to thy loving kindness." Criminals actually took to memorizing this verse. When they came into court, reciting it could save their necks.

The church courts were less interested in punishment than in penance. It was considered un-Christian to order the mutilation or execution of a person who was sorry for his crimes and ready to ask God's forgiveness. Instead, a criminal would perform certain acts to show his sorrow for his sin. A murderer might be stripped of his clothing and forced to march naked across the countryside to pray at a religious shrine; he might be required to eat no meat, to take cold baths, or to flog himself with a whip or chain. Penance for the murder of a bishop, in one instance, involved a 14-year fast of bread and water. Penitents were not always trusted to carry out their own sentences, however. Sometimes they were confined in a monastery, where their prayers and fasting could be supervised by the monks. This custom was the beginning of the idea that imprisonment could lead to the rehabilitation of the prisoner.

As the English kings became more powerful, the influence of the church courts gradually waned. Finally, in the sixteenth century, church justice fell victim to Henry VIII's quarrel with the Pope. Angered because he could not get the Pope's approval for his plan to divorce his Queen and remarry, Henry abolished England's ties with Roman Catholicism and established a new church with himself as the head. This was the end of benefit of clergy, but the notion of rehabilitating criminals did not die. It offered a way to deal—not with murderers, thieves, or arsonists—but with a different sort of criminal—the vagabond.

Sixteenth-century vagabonds were basically destitute, homeless wanderers. We would probably call them the hard-core unemployed. Even today some people have little sympathy

The "drunkard's cloak" prevented the wearer from indulging his habit, and provided the townsfolk with entertainment.

for the poor and out of work, but in Henry VIII's day vaga-
bondage was actually a crime. England was going through a
period of great economic changes, and many landlords were
evicting tenant farmers from lands their families had occupied
for centuries. There was no welfare or unemployment compensation, and homeless farmers were indeed quite likely to turn
to theft in order to keep alive. Many others moved to the cities,
where they became beggars.

Middle-class people lived in fear of the vagabonds. At first,
they tried to deal with the problem by imposing stiff penalties.
One English Poor Law ordered that vagabonds over the age of
14 should be "grievously whipped and burned through the
gristle of the right ear with a hot iron."

Sometimes, however, there were so many homeless and
unemployed that this solution became impractical. In 1557
Bishop Ridley of London complained about the "sturdy vagabonds" roaming the city, and Edward VI donated his old palace
at Bridewell to house the "lewd and idle." This was the first
English House of Correction. The inmates worked at Bridewell: they spun cloth, they baked bread, and some even made
tennis balls. In fact, the institution so impressed Parliament
that in 1576 a law was passed requiring every county in England to follow London's example.

In theory, a House of Correction was a prison for petty
thieves and pickpockets. The old, sick, and destitute were
placed in Workhouses. In practice there was little difference
between a Workhouse and a House of Correction, and both
kinds of inmates were often lumped together in the same
building. This situation reflected the then common belief that
poverty was basically the result of immorality and so not much
different from thieving. Giving former vagabonds and their
families a chance to work, even at the price of their freedom,
was considered quite enlightened.

There was a great deal of enthusiasm for the House of
Corrections in the rest of Europe. In 1669, the efforts of one re-

former in the city of Hamburg, Germany, were remembered in this way:

> Mr. Peter Rentzel . . . Councillor of this town, who experienced many cases in which punishment levied on wrongdoers bore little fruit, really hardening the offenders in their evildoing, conceived the very Christian idea of erecting a Spinnhaus at his own cost . . . so that all such evildoers may be enclosed therein, brought to the fear of God and put to work and saved from . . . damnation.

Note Rentzel's reasons for believing in the *Spinnhaus*. They demonstrate the conviction of these seventeenth-century social activists that "evildoers" could be reformed. It was the first time in European history such a notion had become important outside of church courts. And it was very important, especially to those who felt that harsh laws hadn't worked.

But the expectations of men like Peter Rentzel were not always fulfilled. Too often, Houses of Correction were badly managed; the inmates were hungry and mistreated. And, of course, the system did nothing to resolve the problems that had caused the inmates' sorry condition in the first place.

The creation of Houses of Correction by no means ended the crime problem, and in succeeding centuries other forms of punishment went in and out of favor. In Henry VIII's time, for example, executions were commonplace; some historians estimate that 72,000 people were executed during his reign. That would amount to an average of 2,000 death sentences a year in a country whose population was just a little over 3 million.

Henry's daughter, Queen Elizabeth I, preferred to use convicts as galley slaves to man the oars of English warships. By 1602, galley slaves had become the backbone of the English navy, and Elizabeth appointed a commission to enlarge the list of crimes for which offenders could be sent to the galleys. "Even in their punishment," the practical Queen declared, "they may yield some profitable service to the Commonwealth."

This 17th century gallows at Tyburn was very efficient—three lawbreakers could be hanged at one time and dropped into the burial pit below.

During Elizabeth's reign and after, death penalties were imposed less and less often. By the time Queen Anne died in 1714, there were only 32 *capital crimes*—or crimes punishable by death. It seemed that public opinion was turning against this extreme way of dealing with petty lawbreakers, but only a decade or so later there was a backlash in favor of executions. By 1800, there were once again over 200 capital offenses. Pickpockets, thieves, counterfeiters, and even poachers—those who were caught hunting deer on private lands—were all subject to hanging. (Landscape scenes painted by English artists of this period sometimes show gibbeted corpses—the dead bodies of criminals which were soaked in tar and left hanging in chains as a warning to others.) In London alone, 1,121 people were condemned to death between 1749 and 1771. "There is no regenerating a felon in this life," one judge declared. "For his sake as well as for the sake of society I think it better to hang."

Not everyone agreed. Many judges felt uneasy about imposing the death penalty for minor crimes, and when one young boy was hanged for stealing a loaf of bread there was a public outcry. "So many Christian men and women," mourned the Lord Chief Justice Edward Coke, "[have been] strangled on the cursed tree of the gallows."

Partly as a result of such objections, another form of punishment came into favor—*transportation*. The first law allowing this penalty was passed in 1597, and by 1717 judges were allowed to substitute transportation for any offense "for which [the criminal] is liable to be whipt or burned on the hand."

In a way, transporting, or shipping criminals out of the country, was a return to the age-old punishment of exile. But now there was a convenient place to send large numbers of offenders: the New World. The American colonies needed settlers—men and women who would work the land and fill the little towns which were beginning to dot the eastern seaboard. Why not settle these towns with convicts?

In 1729, a member of Parliament, James Oglethorpe, helped this movement along. One of Oglethorpe's friends, a talented architect, had been sent to prison for going into debt. In those days, debtors were arrested, thrown into confinement, and kept there until they could pay what they owed. It wasn't easy to raise money from inside the gaol. Many debtors thus spent the rest of their lives behind bars. Anyone with wealthy friends could usually manage to borrow enough money to bribe the guards and live fairly comfortably in gaol, but Oglethorpe's friend refused on principle to play this game. He was placed with the poorest prisoners, where he soon caught smallpox and died.

Oglethorpe was shocked. Looking for a way to eliminate

This prisoner's cell is unusually roomy and well-lit for an English gaol.

such tragedies, he asked the king for land in America which could be settled mostly by debtors. King George II granted this request, not out of sympathy, but because he thought that the new colony could act as a buffer between British lands to the north and the Spanish armies in Florida.

Many debtors made a new life in Oglethorpe's colony, which was named Georgia in honor of the king. Usually the

debtors had to sign a contract agreeing to work for as long as
seven years for some landowner already settled in the colony.
Master and servant each kept half of the contract, each half
being known as an *indent*.

Indentured servants were also sent to the other American
colonies. From 1732 to 1776, between 50 and 100,000 people
came to the New World this way.

Then something happened that put an end to the practice
of transportation, at least temporarily: the American Revolution. By 1779, England once again had to find another answer
to the old question: what to do with criminals?

By this time, the English navy had switched to sailing
ships and no longer needed galley slaves. Capital punishment
was no longer considered appropriate for minor crimes. Out of
desperation, people began to take a second look at the gaols.

In the previous 400 years there had been occasional critics
of the English gaol system. In 1593, a committee of the House
of Commons reported that some gaolers were known to "exact
excessive prices for victuals, bedding, fire, fees of irons and
other things from poor prisoners who for want of means . . .
do perish through famine." In 1618, a debtor named Geoffrey
Mynshal had written the first treatise on prison conditions.
And in 1702, the Society for the Promotion of Christian Knowledge produced a report condemning gaols because the old prisoners corrupted the new ones. It criticized the swearing, gambling, promiscuity, and bribery which flourished inside English
gaols.

All of these reports had been ignored. Gaols were considered a necessary evil at best, and they had never been the
primary method of punishment. Now, however, their conditions suddenly became a topic of great interest. Two very different writers, one in Italy and one in England, produced important books on the subject, which were read, praised, and
most important, acted upon, right from their days of publication.

3

The Reformers

In the winter of 1760, society gossip in Milan, Italy, was full of the scandalous behavior of a young nobleman named Cesare Bonesana, the Marchese di Beccaria. Beccaria had defied custom by falling in love with a poor woman. Worse still, he wanted to marry her! His father was so enraged that he had Beccaria arrested.

If anything, this experience seems to have made Beccaria more of a rebel than ever. As soon as he was free, he married the young women he loved, and shortly thereafter joined a club, known as the Academy of the Fists. The club was not devoted to fistfighting, but to reading; its name came from the fierce arguments that sometimes broke out over books.

Beccaria and his friends were not unusual among educated people of the eighteenth century. It was a new age for Europe—the one historians now call the Age of Reason. Old customs and institutions were re-examined; philosophers argued that the calm, detached methods Galileo had used to study the stars and the solar system could now be turned to the study of human beings. In France, especially, there arose a

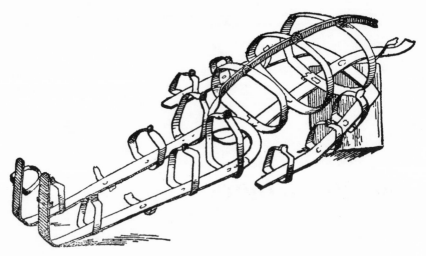

An intricate set of irons for holding prisoners.

whole school of thinkers dedicated to questioning social conventions.

As Beccaria and his friends read the works of these French authors, they had the exhilarating feeling that to understand how society works would make it possible to change things for the better. One book the Academy of the Fists especially admired was the *Spirit of the Laws* by Montesquieu, published in 1748. Montesquieu proposed a thorough revision of the legal code to make the laws more logical and fair.

A few years after his marriage, Beccaria became interested in the question of criminal justice. He had toured the prisons of Milan and was shocked by what he found. And in 1764, urged on by his friends, he wrote a book about it. He called it *An Essay on Crime and Punishment*. Prisoners, especially poor ones, were kept in inhuman conditions, Beccaria argued. Torture was used, both to make suspected criminals confess and to punish the convicted. Punishment was generally out of all proportion to the crime.

"Why do we punish criminals, anyway?" he asked. His answer: to *prevent* them from breaking the law again and to *deter* others from committing the same crime. In short, the criminal's punishment served less as retribution than as an example to others.

For this reason, Beccaria disliked transportation. After all, how could a man 5,000 miles across the ocean serve as any kind of example at all?

Beccaria argued for more use of prison sentences. But he made a point of calling for better treatment of prisoners.

He argued that punishments should fit the crime. If a man knows he will hang either for stealing a pheasant or for murdering a prince, why not murder the prince?

He disapproved of hanging. "Capital punishment cannot be useful because of the example of barbarity it presents," he wrote. "To me it seems an absurdity that the laws, which are an expression of the public will, which abhor and which punish murder, should themselves commit one."

He made many other suggestions: he called for education as a means of preventing crime. He protested against the secrecy which surrounded trials in Italy. He recommended public trials, similar to those in England in which the defendant could face his accuser. He condemned the use of torture. He wrote angrily about the different punishments for rich and poor. He called for "certainty and swiftness" of punishment as the best way to deter criminals.

Beccaria's book was published anonymously. It was less than 100 pages long, but its influence would span continents and centuries. Within the next few months it went into three editions, and the Patriotic Society of Berne awarded its author a gold medal without even knowing who he was, calling Beccaria "a citizen who dared to raise his voice in favor of humanity."

In Austria, the Empress Maria Theresa used the book as a guide to revise her criminal code. After his identity was revealed, Beccaria was asked by Catherine the Great to come to Russia to help with reform in her country. (He didn't go; he didn't like to travel.) And in the United States, both John Adams and Thomas Jefferson read Beccaria and quoted him in their private journals.

Probably the happiest moment for Beccaria came when he learned how his book had excited the philosopers of France. He had written about how much he admired men like Montesquieu and Denis Diderot, the French encyclopedist. Now these men praised him, and the French edition of his book went into seven printings.

Meanwhile, in England, Beccaria's book became a favorite of John Howard, a man who was to become a leader in prison reform both in his country and in America. Howard was 12 years older than Beccaria. Once, as a young man, on a journey to Portugal, he had been aboard a ship captured by French privateers. Howard was thrown in the brig for 40 hours without food or water, and later he was put into a castle dungeon where between beatings he slept on the cold floor and ate bread and water. All his life, Howard would have vivid memories of this miserable experience.

Back in England, Howard led a quiet life, managing the estates he inherited from his father. Then, in 1773, when he was 48 years old, he was appointed Sheriff of Bedfordshire County. At that time few sheriffs paid attention to the gaols except as a source of revenue. Howard did the unthought of: he inspected the entire gaol and visited every inmate.

What he saw disturbed him. Felons were held in a dungeon 11 feet below ground. They slept on wet floors. And when he began to visit gaols in other English towns, he found them, if anything, worse.

He saw prisoners starving. He saw them kept in tiny rooms with little air and no water. Howard saw the tyranny of officials extorting every possible penny from prisoners. He saw debtors thrown in the same room with brutal murderers. He saw innocent men and women spending years of their lives alongside the worst criminals in the country.

He hated the degrading make-work which had been invented for convicts as part of their punishment, like oakum picking, which meant plucking out rope fibers by hand from old, tar-soaked rope. This dreary job was forced on prisoners

John Howard's gaol inspections were legendary. Here he's shown "relieving a prisoner."

throughout England. Some gaols even forced prisoners to spend their days carrying rocks from one end of a yard to the other and back again.

Howard's tours of inspection became an obsession. In 1776, he began a tour through Europe. Always a careful recorder, Howard later figured that he traveled 13,418 miles—no mean feat in the days of carriages and sailing ships. He visited every prison he could find.

Most other countries were as bad or worse than his own. But in Holland, Howard saw prisoners locked up, not to await punishment as was still usually the case in England, but as a means of punishment. Moreover, these prisoners were put to practical work cleaning streets, repairing highways, or cutting stone. The Dutch prisons were cleaner than most. The food

The British prison ship, SUCCESS, toured the globe as an "educational object lesson" to law-abiding citizens.

was decent. And prisoners who were well behaved were let loose before their terms were over.

His experience in Holland was a pleasant surprise: here were convicted lawbreakers who seemed to be leading useful lives. He decided that there was much in the Dutch system that could be adopted in England.

In 1777, Howard wrote and published a book describing prison conditions and offering his suggestions as to how they might be improved. *The State of Prisons* called for many reforms: individual cells for prisoners, adequate rations, and medical care. He wanted to separate debtors from felons, men from women, the insane from the sane. Howard was determined that his book should be read and acted upon: he gave away hundreds of copies, mostly to people who had influence in the government.

People were ready to listen. The American Revolution had ended England's policy of transportation and the Crown was at a loss for ways to deal with criminals. Confinement was beginning to seem the obvious answer, but there was no room for all of England's convicts in the existing prisons and gaols.

Already, in 1776, an interim answer had been reached. An old warship, the *Justitia,* was tied up in the Thames river and used to house convicts. The prisoners worked at projects like deepening the river channel and cleaning the river bed.

In succeeding years more such ships were set up. They were called the *hulks* and became notorious as floating hell-holes. Prisoners were fed a little moldy cheese, dried peas, and some bread which was half straw. They were given a jacket, a pair of pants, and a shirt, clothing which had to last, day and night, as long as they were aboard.

The prisoners were marched ashore each morning under an armed guard. They worked in chains, watched by men holding drawn cutlasses. They were not fed at all during the day. One writer reports the prisoners thought it was a great privilege to be able to stop work for a minute and drink some dirty water out of a ditch.

As early as 1777, Howard protested conditions aboard the *Justitia.* Few people were willing to defend the hulks—the ships were basically a standby measure. What was needed was a new prison system, a system that would embody some of the principles outlined by Beccaria and by Howard.

In 1779, Parliament passed the Criminal Justice Act calling for the establishment of such a system. The wording of the act shows how readily politicians accepted the new notion that prison could have a reforming effect on the prisoner and was the proper consequence for most crimes. "[If criminals] were ordered to solitary imprisonment," it states, "accompanied by well-regulated labour and religious instruction, it might be the means . . . not only of deterring others from the commission of like crimes but also of reforming the individuals."

By "solitary imprisonment" the English legislators did not mean the kind of absolute isolation modern penologists mean by the phrase: they meant that each prisoner should have a separate cell and that an attempt should be made to prevent prisoners from corrupting each other. The act called for the construction of two "Penitentiary Houses" with separate cells. (It was one of the first times the word *penitentiary*—literally, an institution which would cause people to be sorry—had appeared in print.) John Howard was appointed Supervisor of Buildings.

The act looked like a landmark piece of lawmaking. But the whole plan broke down in personal bickering over the best site for the first penitentiary. Within a year, Howard had resigned from his post. There was no one else committed enough to take his place. It was 12 years before prisons came again to the attention of the legislature.

Howard went right back to inspecting prisons and producing new editions of his book, never letting up until he died in 1790, far from home, from an infection caught in a Russian prison. Meanwhile, for want of anything better, the hulks flourished. By 1825, there were 5,000 convicts afloat in English waters, and the hulks were not abolished until 1857. Also, in 1787 England began transporting convicts again.

This time, they were sent to a new land: Australia, which had only recently been charted by Captain James Cook. On May 13, 1787, a fleet of 11 English ships sailed to Botany Bay, Australia. The trip took eight months. The 552 male and 190 female criminals aboard were the first of over 135,000 convicts sent to the continent between that year and 1875.

Some historians feel the indentured servants in America led reasonably comfortable lives. None have any good words for conditions in Botany Bay and the other Australian penal colonies. Stories of prison camps are filled with descriptions of chain gangs, brutal floggings, and convicts forced into homosexuality.

One convict, Ralph Rashliegh, wrote about his experiences in a lime-burning camp in the mid-nineteenth century.

All the convicts slept outside—some on beds of seaweed, others on bare ground. They wore the same clothes winter and summer. Usually Rashliegh would work 15 hours each day, loading boats as he stood in water as high as his chest. When they weren't being whipped by guards, the convicts fought among themselves for food. Once, Rashliegh was nearly killed when a friend, crazed by hunger, picked up a rake and hit him over the head in a fight over a meatless piece of bone. At the time, however, the Austrialian prison camps received little public attention—they were too far away.

Howard's resignation didn't quite kill the movement for the establishment of a national prison system in England. In fact, the problem attracted the interest of the philosopher, Jeremy Bentham. Convinced that criminals would reform, given isolation and time to reflect, Bentham designed a radically new kind of prison building.

Convicts on prison ships led miserable lives; note the shackles on their wrists and ankles.

He called it the Panopticon. (The word *panopticon* means
see-all.) It was to be an eight-sided building, with cells filling
each wall. Each of the 1,000 inmates would have a cell with a
work area, and he would be alone all the time. But he would be
watched constantly—by guards he couldn't see. There was to
be a system of periscopes which would allow the guard, without moving from his room in the center of the building, to
watch all the prisoners at their work.

Outsiders were to be encouraged to visit the Panopticon.
Bentham had even invented a system of tubes by which visitors might be able to ask each prisoner how he was getting
along.

It would be a lonely life for the prisoners when visitors
weren't around. But Bentham thought being alone would give
them plenty of time to think about why they had gone wrong.
Also, his scheme would keep them away from other prisoners
who might lead them back into evil ways. Bentham called the
Panopticon "a mill for grinding rogues honest, and idle men in-
dustrious."

The plan impressed a lot of people. In 1794, the government made Bentham a grant of 2,000 pounds to start construction. But again, there were problems finding a site, and red
tape kept the scheme tied up for 17 years.

Meanwhile, some people in the government who had
never liked the idea began to speak up. One of them, when he
first saw the plans, had exclaimed, "Yes, there's the keeper—
the spider in his web!" In 1811, a Parliamentary committee
looked into the scheme again and reported against it, on the
grounds that it would give the unseen prison officials a sinister
power over the lives of the inmates. Bentham retreated in
disgust and frustration. However, he lived to see the English
build a number of prisons—one on the exact site of the Panopticon—using many of his ideas.

Bentham also lived to see a sharp decline in capital punishment. In 1822, thanks to him and other reformers, the

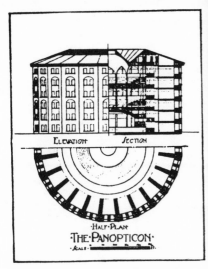

A diagram of the Panopticon.   Jeremy Bentham.

death penalty was abolished for about 100 petty crimes in England.

Instead, judges were sending more people to prison. In Howard's day, they had handed down about 2,000 prison sentences a year. From 1810 to 1817, 56,208 men and women received prison sentences. During the next seven years, the number rose to over 92,000.

Bentham and the other reformers won on the question: where should we send those who break the law? Always before, prisons had been used to hold people until a judge punished them. For the first time, the prison sentence was being used extensively as a punishment in England.

But now, with so many people behind bars, other questions became important. What should be done with lawbreakers once they were in prison? Should they be alone or together? Should they work or remain idle? How should they be punished for misbehavior? How could they be given religious training?

The answers to these questions came not from English reformers but from a city across the ocean. In Philadelphia, reformers were changing the Walnut Street Jail in ways that would earn their state the title Father of the Penitentiary System.

4

"The Prisoner has the Advantage"

The year is 1787. The Walnut Street Jail in Philadelphia is holding its first religious service. A gunner stands in back of the minister, holding a lighted match, ready to fire his cannon if the prisoners riot.

This seems to be a strange way to teach Christianity. But the early reformers in America wanted prisoners to get religion even if it meant aiming cannons at their heads. Introducing Sunday sermons was one of the first official acts of the Philadelphia Society for Alleviating the Miseries of Public Prisons. This society was organized by the Quakers, a religious group whose strong beliefs in nonviolence, tolerance, and salvation led them to approach lawbreakers differently.

As early as 1682, the first Assembly of the Quaker colony of Pennsylvania had adopted a set of laws regulating prisons. The Quakers rejected capital punishment. Their new laws, probably for the first time in history, called for imprisonment at hard labor as punishment for most crimes. The Quakers followed these laws until 1718, when the English government forced them to revert to the whippings, hangings, and assorted cruelties common in England and the other American colonies.

The decades after the American Revolution brought changes in the justice system throughout the new nation. The early settlers had punished petty thieves by locking them up in the stocks. They felt that being laughed at by friends and neighbors for a day or so, would humiliate the lawbreaker so that he would be unlikely to repeat his crime. By 1790, American reformers were questioning the value of such public punishments: what was the point of stocks in a large city like Boston where the community was too large to take much notice of an individual offender? At the same time, the victory over England freed prison reformers to criticize the harsh punishments that had been imposed by their former rulers.

Like the English, Americans were searching for a new approach to punishments and the Quakers of Pennsylvania led the way. In 1776, Pennsylvania called for the reform of penal law. They moved quickly to substitute milder forms of punishment for the whip and hangman's noose. The new laws returned to the Quaker emphasis on prisons in which lawbreakers would receive strong doses of hard work and religion. They also reflected the Quaker belief in the importance of silent meditation. If meditation was good for everyone, surely it was even more important for convicts. The less a prisoner talked to other lawbreakers the better.

And so, in the years after the new laws were passed, there were many changes at Walnut Street. Debtors were separated from felons. Men were separated from women. In 1798, a school was opened. In 1808, the prison officials decided that "prisoners who conduct themselves properly and are diligent in their work" could have visits from members of their families.

But the big change was ordered by the legislature in 1790:

a suitable number of cells . . . each of which cells should be separated from the common yard by walls of such height as without unnecessary exclusion of air and light will prevent all external communication, for the purpose of confining therein the more hardened and atrocious offenders who . . . have been sentenced to hard labour for a term of years.

From now on, the "hardened" criminals would not keep each other company. They would spend most of their time alone. And that was only a beginning. By 1818, the Walnut Street Jail was overcrowded. The Pennsylvania legislature ordered two giant new penitentiaries built. One, Western Penitentiary, would be in Pittsburgh and the other, Eastern, at Philadelphia.

Eastern Penitentiary opened in 1829. Built on what was once a cherry orchard, it came to be called Cherry Hill. It was a massive building. The seven cell blocks, sticking out from the center like spokes in a wheel, contained over 400 cells.

In 1831, shortly after the first nine prisoners had been received, the report of the warden and inspectors described the Cherry Hill system:

> When a convict first arrives he is placed in a cell and left alone without work and without any book. His mind can only operate on itself; generally but a few hours elapse before he petitions for something to do and for a Bible. If the prisoner has a trade that can be pursued in his cell, he is put to work as a favour; as a reward for good behavior . . . a Bible is allowed him. If he has no trade, or one that cannot be pursued in his cell, he is allowed to choose one that can and he is instructed by one of the overseers.

At Cherry Hill, each prisoner was completely alone. He never spoke to another prisoner—or even saw one. He was brought into the prison blindfolded. He ate, worked, and slept alone for many years—sometimes until he died.

The system of Cherry Hill became known as the "separate system." Some people were very excited about it; others thought it cruel. When Charles Dickens visited America, he visited Cherry Hill hoping to find ideas he could carry back to England. He wrote, instead, "In its intention I am well convinced that it is kind . . . but . . . very few men are capable of estimating the immense amount of torture and agony which this dreadful punishment, prolonged for years, inflicts upon sufferers."

The 7-spoked "wheel" design of Cherry Hill made it as formidable as a fortress.

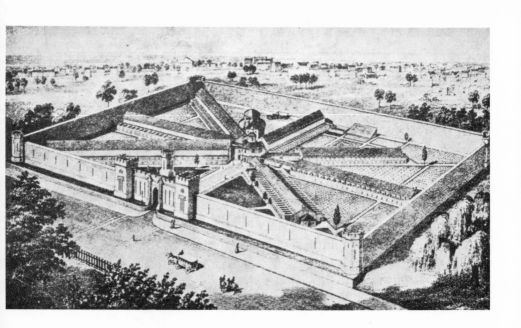

Meanwhile, a different sort of penitentiary evolved in Auburn, New York. At Auburn, each prisoner slept in his own cell, a small, unheated room with little light, and he also stayed there whenever he was not working.

The difference was that at Auburn the prisoners worked together. There were large workshops. Each day the prisoners walked in what has been called a "slow motion shuffle," or "lock-step," each inmate with a hand on the shoulder of the man in front, into the shops where they worked side by side. The New York prison officials did not want lawbreakers to talk to each other any more than the Quakers did. Prisoners had to be absolutely silent. If a prisoner so much as whispered a single word to the man sitting next to him, he would be flogged.

The Auburn system became known as the "silent system." One reformer described the silent system in action, during meals. "Not a whisper is heard . . . The convicts are seated at narrow tables with their backs towards the center, so that there can be no interchange of signs. If one has more food than he wants, he raises his left hand and if another has less he raises his right hand and the waiter changes it."

A great battle arose between those who believed in the separate system of Pennsylvania and those who believed in the silent or "congregate" system of Auburn.

"The Pennsylvania system is cruel," some reformers said. "It is so lonely for prisoners it breeds insanity."

"The New York system is crueler," others shot back. "To put prisoners in the same room and not allow them to talk is to tempt them in a very unfair way."

Magazines would poll foreign visitors or distinguished Americans and print their opinions on the controversy. Pamphlets, articles, and books streamed from groups like the Boston Prison Discipline Society, which favored the silent system. There were stinging replies from groups on the other side, like the Philadelphia Society for Alleviating the Miseries of Public Prisons. The debate lasted for more than 30 years.

Under the "silent system" that originated at Auburn, New York, prisoners marched to meals in lock-step.

The battle seems a little puzzling today. On the important points both sides thought alike. Both believed that capital punishment and use of the whip were cruel punishments and that imprisonment was the best way to deal with lawbreakers. Both believed that prisons would deter people from a life of crime and would *rehabilitate* those who were sent there.

They also believed in what one historian has called "the trinity around which officials organized the penitentiary": the three ideas of *separation, obedience,* and *labor.* At both Auburn and Philadelphia, the prisoners could not talk to each other. They had to obey prison officials. And they had to work hard.

There was one advantage to the congregate prison at Auburn, especially for politicians eager to keep taxes low. It was cheaper. There was no need for the private exercise yards and large individual work spaces of the separate system. Prison labor could be organized more efficiently and profitably when the workers were not segregated. Prisoners could be kept in small cells.

So, as the states built penitentiaries, most of them imitated the one at Auburn. Connecticut built a congregate prison at Wethersfield. Congregate prisons were built in Illinois. And when Iowa decided to build a prison, they sent a man east to study the Auburn model.

Nineteenth-century prison officials found that the products of prison labor could be sold outside at a profit. Prisoners were paid for their work, but they were also charged for their food, clothes, and lodging. Through the nineteenth century, most American prisons were self-supporting and even had money left over.

Guards shared in what profits there were. Prison officials reasoned that the guards would encourage the prisoners to work, and while the state (and the taxpayers) benefited from the profits, the prisoners would benefit still more from the spiritual discipline of labor.

But guards became obsessed with profits. They pushed the prisoners to produce. The silent system, which had been devised with the good of the prisoner in mind—to save him from being corrupted by the criminals who surrounded him— became a tool to help the guards run the workshops. Also, the floggings and tortures which prison sentences were supposed to replace now began to find their way back as punishments for breaking intricate and oppressive rules.

One side effect of the congregate system was that public awareness of prisons declined. Prisoners were usually not allowed to have visitors, or if they were, the visitors rarely got to see the cells and work areas where the convicts actually spent their time. In general, the taxpayers were happy that the prisons paid for themselves and were willing to believe the wildly optimistic claims made by prison officials. "Could we all be put on prison fare, for the space of two generations," wrote

Reverend James B. Finley, chaplain of the Ohio penitentiary, "the world would ultimately be better for it."

Despite the reverend's enthusiasm, it is doubtful that anyone would have wanted to change places with a prisoner. True, health conditions were far better than those in the English gaols of 400 years before. Men and women were no longer thrown together. Debtors were no longer behind bars. And most important, the prisoners were no longer waiting for punishment—their sentence itself *was* the punishment.

Yet the prisons themselves were fortresslike stone buildings with thick walls and high turrets. They were supposed to look frightening, and they did. And the inmates led lives that were completely controlled by prison officials. Imagine following this typical nineteenth-century prison routine every day for years: early in the morning a bell sounded or a horn rang. Keepers opened the cell doors, and prisoners, wearing striped

In the 19th century, prison industries like hat-making were productive and profitable.

uniforms, marched one behind the other out to the yard. They carried night pails—still in use in the many twentieth-century prisons without toilets in the cells. After emptying the pails and putting them on racks to dry, the inmates headed for work-shops. There they sat on long benches, working at looms or other simple machines until another bell rang.

Breakfast! Single file, the prisoners headed for the kitchen to pick up a tray or a tin of food. They ate, then returned to the shops for work, stopping for lunch and dinner.

At six, without having spoken a word all day, they marched back to the cells where they had only a cot, the night pail, and some tin utensils. There they could read the Bible—but nothing else. Lights went out at nine.

Who were the prisoners who followed this deadening rou-tine?

The average prisoner was poor and uneducated. Often he was an immigrant. By 1850, 32% of the inmates at the New York State prisons of Sing Sing, Clinton, and Auburn were foreign born. And by 1861, the percentage was 44%. The in-creasing number of immigrant convicts placed an even greater strain on the relationship between prisoners and their guards and isolated the prisoners all the more.

Some prisoners fared better than others. In Connecticut, Warden Amos Pilsbury decided that inmates he trusted, called "trusties," would be allowed to go into the town by themselves to shop or run errands. Pilsbury's "trustie system" was much copied. But it was also abused, especially when trusties were given guns and allowed to act as guards. There were cases of trusties who would talk prisoners into escaping, so they could shoot them as they ran away and so gain credit with prison of-ficials.

All too often, prison administrators were cruel—and some were monstrously cruel. If an inmate was caught whispering a word to the man next to him at dinner—even after a whole day of silence—he met some horrible punishment. Prisoners were sometimes stripped naked and whipped. In one prison, the guards enjoyed shooting hard jets of water at the wrongdoer until "blood burst from the eyes and ears."

By the late 1800's, prison wardens had developed some new punishments, unheard of even in the old days before "reform." California prison guards, according to one record, would take a 4-foot long strip of canvas and wrap it around a prisoner's body so tightly that the laces cut his skin. Then, sometimes for as long as four days, they would kick, beat, or bounce the helpless convict as if he were a soccer ball.

Naturally, prison reformers were shocked to see how their well-meaning theories had worked out in practice. "Was it necessary to be so cruel?" they asked. But the wardens, burdened with enforcing so many rules and keeping order inside prison walls, had lost sight of the goals of rehabilitation. "We have enough trouble keeping them quiet," was their reply to most suggestions about improving the lot of the convicts.

By the 1850's, many Americans were changing their minds about prisons. Crime was as much a problem as ever. The ideas which had originated at Cherry Hill obviously hadn't made much difference. Even the New York Prison Commission was disillusioned, and in 1852, it reported that "protracted incarceration destroys the better faculties of the soul."

Two well-known prison reformers agreed. In 1867, they wrote, disappointedly, "There is not a state prison in America in which the reformation of the convicts is the one supreme object."

☞ *5*

The New Sciences

In 1889, more than a century after the appearance of Beccaria's book, another Italian, a doctor named Cesare Lombroso, published a book called *The Criminal Man*. Lombroso suggested that there was a connection between certain physical characteristics and the tendency to break the law. He believed robbers, for example, had snub noses, thin beards, and receding foreheads. "Habitual homicides," he wrote, "have glassy, motionless eyes, sometimes bloodshot and infected. The nose is often aquiline or rather hawklike, and always voluminous."

Working with ideas derived from Charles Darwin, whose theory of evolution had been published about 30 years before, he developed the notion that criminals were evolutionary "throwbacks" to a more primitive species of man and could be identified by their physical resemblance to the apes.

It sounds crazy. But as wrong as Lombroso's theories may have been, his methods were revolutionary. With tape measure and notebook, he made careful physical studies of thousands of convicted lawbreakers. Because he tried to base his conclusions on his observations, he was approaching the question of crime from a new angle: scientific rather than religious or philosophical.

By modern standards of scientific research, of course, Lombroso was nowhere near careful enough. He didn't do control experiments on the law-abiding population. But though Lombroso's theory and methods have been discredited, his example encouraged other scientists to follow him into the prisons. Some of his successors were doctors and psychologists; others belonged to a new scientific discipline, social science. Like Lombroso, they made physical studies of the prisoners. They also collected information on prisoners' past histories, family background, and social development.

Armed with the results of their observations, this new generation of social scientists came to believe that crime was a complex matter and that they would never find a single way to reform lawbreakers. "Each lawbreaker is a unique human being," the social scientists agreed. "We should treat each one differently."

After all, weren't some prisoners religious and others atheists? Weren't some violent and others too timid to raise a fist? Weren't there rich and poor thieves? Criminals who had loving parents and those who had none? Professionals and first offenders? Sane and insane?

In 1843, even before Lombroso had begun his investigations, this point of view won a hearing with the trial of an Englishman named Daniel McNaughton. McNaughton had killed the secretary of a well-known English politician, but at the trial he insisted that he had killed the politician himself. By this time, English judges could let a criminal go if he seemed to be suffering from a "delusion." McNaughton clearly was, so he was acquitted.

There was a huge uproar. But the judges held firm. They insisted a man could plead insanity if he "did not know the nature and the quality of the act he was doing, or if he did know it, that he did not know he was doing what was wrong."

The problem of deciding which defendants are insane under the law and which are not remains one of the most vexing issues in modern courtrooms. But the so-called Mc-Naughton rule established a principle that is followed to this day. It was a clear victory for the principle that different law-breakers demanded different treatment.

While judges were beginning to consider the mental state of accused men and women before convicting and sentencing them, prison administrators were toying with the idea of treating convicted prisoners as individuals. Oddly enough, this new plan got its start on Norfolk Island, Australia, a notoriously brutal English penal colony.

In 1840, when Captain Alexander Maconochie was appointed director of Norfolk Island, the prison's reputation as a hellhole was so well established that some convicts drowned themselves rather than face its horrors. In addition, the English practice of transportation was under heavy attack from other Australian settlers who did not want their country used as a dumping ground for criminals. Among the reforms Maconochie introduced was a system that would offer rewards to the better behaved and more cooperative prisoners. Convicts could now earn credits for good behavior in the form of "marks." A prisoner who put in a hard day's work, for example, could earn ten marks. He then had a choice between spending these marks on extra food, or saving them up to buy his freedom.

"When a man keeps the key to his own prison," Maconochie said, "he is soon persuaded to fit it to the lock."

Maconochie was fired after four years of controversy over his reforms. Directors who succeeded him went back to the old system. But by 1853, Walter Crofton, Chairman of the Board of Directors for Convict Prisons in Ireland was developing Maconochie's ideas. Under Crofton's administration, an Irish prisoner spent nine months in solitary. Then he went to work on the roads or digging ditches, and afterward entered a five-step program designed to lead to his discharge. If he was cooperative, he climbed the steps quickly. At one point in the program, he was given a job where he could work with no one watching.

When he was released, the prisoner was given a "ticket of leave," which could be revoked if he misbehaved during the next ten years.

In America, a new generation of reformers read the articles and books written by Maconochie, Crofton, and their supporters. They traveled to Ireland to inspect Crofton's facilities with their own eyes and returned impressed.

It was 1870.

The Civil War was over. Many American civic leaders had devoted their days to raising and financing a giant army and to deciding issues of war, peace, and reconstruction. Now they had energy to tackle some of the problems of peacetime.

That year, prison officials and other people interested in reform met at a national Prison Congress in Cincinnati, Ohio. They formed the National Prison Association. And they adopted a Declaration of Principles, 37 paragraphs long.

Much of it was based on the writings of people like Maconochie. The reformers in Cincinnati no longer believed in the silent system. They wanted American prisons to adopt the "ticket of leave,"; parole, and the indeterminate sentence, a new name for the Maconochie system of adjusting a sentence for good behavior. They wanted prisoners taught trades which they could use after they were out of prison. "Reformation, not vindictive suffering," they wrote, "should be the purpose of penal treatment."

It was ironic. Almost 100 years earlier the act calling for creation of penitentiaries in England had included the very same goal of reformation. Nevertheless, there were still many who opposed the plan of that 1870 convention, especially prison officials in the South. There, the chain gang was a common sight on rural roads: a dozen or more men, chained together at the ankles, swinging pickaxes for 12 hours at a stretch, guards with whips and guns standing constant watch. Even in the late 1930s, Southerners would defend this system. "It kept men out of doors in God's open country," one southern senator said, "where they could enjoy the singing of birds."

Convict labor helped build the New Orleans Pacific Railroad.

But, especially up North, the reformers made headway.

In 1876, the New York Legislature passed a law setting up a reformatory at Elmira, New York, for young men 16 to 30 years of age. None of the offenders would serve a fixed sentence. Instead, depending upon their behavior, the board of managers would decide when they were eligible for parole.

The idea of a reformatory for juveniles wasn't totally new. A rich New Yorker had founded a House of Refuge for the young as early as 1825. By 1857, there were 17 reformatories in the United States. They housed over 20,000 juveniles.

Elmira, though, was different. Zebulon Brockway, who first directed the Elmira Reformatory, had been very impressed by Crofton's Irish system. But he did not believe in that first nine months of solitary confinement. What's more, he made sure Elmira had a library, gym, athletic field, and glee club. In 1883, Elmira became the first prison in America to have a newspaper written by inmates. Citizens from the town were asked to come into the prison to teach trades like telegraphy and printing.

Brockway's high hopes for Elmira were not fulfilled. Part of the problem was that he couldn't get specially trained personnel to run his educational program. It was hard to convince the young inmates that education was something other than punishment when it was thrust at them by surly prison guards. Morale at Elmira declined quickly, till it seemed no more than a "junior prison." And evidence that boys who had been through Elmira were less likely to commit crimes than ones who had been sentenced before 1876 and sent to ordinary prisons proved impossible to find.

Still, the Elmira Reformatory had shown that it was possible to separate young lawbreakers from adult professional criminals and treat them differently. Now other states began setting up categories of prisoners and trying to find different ways of handling each. In 1873, Indiana created the first separate prison for females. Since colonial days, men and women had been kept in the same buildings, but their quarters had been separate from those of the men. Now states began to feel that women did not have to be treated as harshly as men. Massachusetts built a Women's Reformatory in 1877, and others followed soon after.

There were also changes in architecture—the way prisons were built and looked. In the nineteenth century, states were happy with the "fortress" prison with its high thick walls. In 1916, the Lorton Virginia Reformatory for the District of Columbia became the first penal institution without walls in the United States. Prison officials began to talk about *minimum security* and *maximum security* prisons.

"Why lock up the prisoners we can trust?" they asked. And states like California and New York built prisons without walls for them.

Many states began to *classify* prisoners. They separated the man who was in for the first time from the hardened criminal—often giving each type of prisoner a different uniform or braid on his trousers.

The psychologist became more important in prison work. World War I had seen the prestige of this new field increase. When the U.S. Army examined every soldier to see if he was fit for duty, tests written by psychiatrists and psychologists were used. They found they could predict accurately how a soldier would behave under stress. Prison officials concluded that psychologists might also have some insights about convicts.

So, after World War I, many prisons added psychologists to their staffs. They tested prisoners and counseled them. Prisons in many states set up what were called *diagnostic clinics*. When a prisoner was first admitted to prison, he or she would talk to a group of prison officials that might include the warden, a doctor, the chaplain, and the psychologists. They would decide what kinds of programs in the prison were best for the new inmate.

There were also changes in education and job training. Prison officials began to provide more nutritious diets for prisoners. Medical care became more thorough. And prisoners were allowed to talk to each other as they sat at mealtime or at work.

In 1905, the warden at the Michigan State Penitentiary had begun allowing prisoners some say in how the prison was run. For a while, especially in New York, other prisons experimented with this new idea—that prisoners might govern themselves.

But every time one problem receded, another arose. In the 1930's, for example, prison work programs ran into difficulties. Free industry had always resisted the competition from prison-manufactured goods. Now that the depression was on, there was strong public feeling against giving convicts paying work when honest men outside were jobless. Gradually, most states passed laws forbidding the sale of prison-made goods that competed with products made by free men. This meant prison industry was no longer profitable, and in many cases, the work programs simply died.

Racial tension surfaced in prisons. By the 1960's, the majority of the inmates in northern prisons were black or Puerto Rican; the guards, on the other hand, were white as guards had always been. And, by the end of the 1960's, many state prisons were powder kegs of racial hostility and frustration.

Then, on September 9, 1971, inmates of Attica prison in New York State, arming themselves with clubs, sticks, rakes, and knives, poured into tunnels leading to the cell block gates. They overpowered guards and took control of the prison. For four days they controlled the five cell blocks, six other buildings, and the prison yard. They held 43 prison staff members hostage. They made an immediate demand for amnesty: "Freedom for all and from all physical, mental and legal reprisal."

They also demanded 28 changes designed to make prison life bearable—better food, decent medical care, more black and Spanish-speaking guards, the right to receive mail without its being censored, the right to receive visits from friends. Even many of the prison officials felt the demands were reasonable.

But the state commissioner was not willing to grant the prisoners' demands at gunpoint. On the rainy morning of September 13, as prisoners sat drying themselves over campfires in the yard, troopers armed with rifles and shotguns gathered in front of the administration building. The prisoners refused to release the hostages. In fact, they blindfolded them and moved them to the catwalks holding knives to their throats.

At 9:44 A.M., National Guard helicopters dropped gas into the yard. The riflemen opened fire. After four minutes, 10 hostages and 19 inmates were dying—all from police bullets. Three hostages and 85 inmates suffered bullet wounds.

What happened? After a hundred years of changes are American prisons still unbearable for their inmates?

The disaster at Attica shocked the world of corrections. New York State set up a special committee to find out why the

Inmates raise their fists in protest during the Attica uprising in 1971.

Attica after the uprising; inmates waiting to be strip searched lie face down, their hands locked behind their heads.

inmates were prepared to risk their lives to protest. After the committee reported, many changes were made in the state prison system. The cagelike grills in the visiting rooms were taken down, and friends were allowed to visit where only immediate family had been permitted before. The rules governing clothing, mail, and possessions were relaxed. New work and education programs were started to allow prisoners more time away from their cells. And the state began a determined recruitment program to get black and Hispanic guards into the system.

The reforms went too far—and not far enough. The old guards resented the new system—they believed that the prisoners were there for punishment. And their resentment grew when new minority guards came on the job. Racial tension in prisons had been serious before, but now it was guard against guard.

With the new rules, security was harder to maintain. For example, the new freedom in the visiting room made it much easier for visitors to smuggle drugs and weapons into prison. To control smuggling, more guards had to be hired, and that strained the corrections budget.

This time disillusionment with the reforms set in more quickly than ever. In the summer of 1977, the recently appointed New York State Commissioner of the Department of Correctional Services, Benjamin Ward, started to cut back on the new programs and to encourage a return to the old tough discipline. One of his deputies put it this way: "All we have discovered about rehabilitation is that we are not doing it. . . . Let us begin to focus on cost."

And so the history of prison goes. Separate cells, hard labor, transportation, the reformatory, classification, diagnostic clinics: each new idea looked like the answer . . . for a while. And each generation of reformers entered their careers in penology excited and hopeful . . . and retired in despair and disillusionment. "We thought it would work," they would say when they wrote their memoirs, 30 or 40 years later.

Could the problem lie, not with the details of prison life but with the very idea of imprisonment?

After all, the prison sentence was first embraced by reformers because it seemed more humane than hanging and flogging. They were guided by their sense of decency and justice—not by any real knowledge of what causes people to become thieves and murderers or what would keep them from stealing or killing again.

It's only since Lombroso that sociologists, criminologists, and penologists in America and around the world have been systematically studying the prisoner, the prison system, and the effect of imprisonment on the individual.

To an increasing number of these experts, the prison system is a disaster. They feel that the theories of Beccaria, Howard, the Philadelphia prison society, even Manonochie and Crofton, encouraged the growth of a system which is simply a terrible mistake. They argue that it is unfair, especially to poor people and blacks, that it is cruel—even that it may lead to more crime.

The following chapters will look at some of their reasons. And—first things first—we will begin by looking at the steps of the American criminal justice system which precede going to prison.

Inmate photo, Sing Sing.

6

How Do They Get There?

The three of them drove around town until it got dark. Then they parked and walked toward the gas station, Tina carrying a brown paper bag in one hand.

When they stepped inside, she took her gun from the bag and pointed it at the attendant's head. "This is a stickup," she said. "Give me all the money you have."

He didn't argue. He opened the safe and handed over $64. Still holding the gun to his head, Tina forced him into the back room and locked the door. Then she and her friends fled.

She is still angry that she was caught.

"My girl friend told on me," she says now. "The one that did it with me. She got picked up for curfew. She was high, and she just ran off at the mouth."

Like Tina, many prisoners are angry when they are caught. They blame it on luck or their accomplices. They feel that most criminals get away with their crime.

It is hard to feel sorry for someone who makes a habit of pointing guns at people. But in blaming luck for her arrest, Tina has a point.

"Crime," write Edwin Sutherland and Donald Cressey in their classic *Principles of Criminology*, "is much more general and pervasive than the ordinary statistics indicate. Opposition to the law has been a tradition in the United States." To support their point, they remind the reader of Shay's Rebellion of 1787, the whiskey insurrection in 1794, slave-trading *and* the harboring of runaway slaves, and violation of prohibition. They point to celebrations—New Years' Eve, football parades—during which lawbreaking is often ignored.

They also quote the well-known work of two researchers, James Wallenstein and Clement Lyle, who in 1947 surveyed 1,700 affluent adults who had never been arrested for anything. A staggering 91% of them had committed at least one serious crime. *Most* of the men—64%—had committed one felony; 26% had stolen cars.

Sutherland at one point, studied 70 large American corporations. Over a 40-year period, every one of them had violated at least one major federal law concerning restraint of trade, misrepresentation in advertising, patent infringement, or financial fraud. The average number of violations totaled 13 per company.

Most lawbreakers never see a prison cell. In fact, one federal official quoted by Jessica Mitford put it this way: "Of 100 major crimes, 50 are reported to the police. For 50 incidents reported, 12 persons are arrested. Of the 12 arrested, 6 are convicted of anything—not necessarily of the offense reported. Of the 6 who are convicted, 1.5 go to prison or jail."

For some, such a summary proves that the American system of criminal justice is a complete failure. It looks as if almost everybody can get away with breaking the law.

In fact, such figures only tell part of the story.

It is true that the odds are against the police arresting someone who breaks the law once. But those who make a practice of breaking the law are usually caught at some point.

And, while it is true that only a small percentage of those

Inmate photo, Green Haven State Prison; New York.

arrested are sent to prison, that is not necessarily the failure of the criminal justice system.

After all, some suspects are innocent. Others are acquitted because their victims refuse to testify. This is particularly true, Charles Silberman points out, in the case of crimes involving friends or relatives. After all, a family whose car has been "borrowed" by an uncle may not want him prosecuted.

Furthermore, the great bulk of suspects who do not go to prisons are juveniles, although more and more states are passing legislation which makes juveniles who commit certain violent crimes subject to the same sentences as adults.

Let's look briefly at what happens to the accused before being convicted and put behind bars.

Tina's first contact with the criminal justice system came with her talk with the policeman who brought her in for questioning.

By "police" we may mean enforcement officers hired by a number of governmental bodies. A city usually has a police force. So may the county. The federal government concentrates its police work in the Federal Bureau of Investigation, though there are other federal enforcement agencies.

In this case it was a county deputy sheriff who found Tina. If she had been a juvenile, Tina would have been sent home or to a specialized juvenile center. If she had money to put up as assurance she would show up for trial—bail—she would have been released. But she was an adult and did not have the money for bail. She waited for her trial in the county jail.

And there she met with a lawyer assigned to her by the state to decide how to handle yet another part of the criminal justice system: criminal court.

Should Tina ask for a jury trial? For reasons we will explore later, she decided to plead guilty in front of a judge. The length of time he ordered her to stay at Dwight constituted her *sentence.*

Sentences are designed to fit the crime. Tina was a felon. *Felonies* include some pretty serious crimes—rape, assault, and burglary, for example. In all states, a felony is punished by more than one year in a state or federal prison.

When Tina's friend was picked up for curfew violation, she was a misdemeanant. *Misdemeanors* are minor crimes. A drunk passes out in the street. A teenager smokes a joint. A woman shoplifts a pair of sunglasses. All have committed misdemeanors.

These minor criminals don't go to prison. Usually they appear before a local judge, and he makes them pay a fine or serve a relatively short term in the city jail.

A few crimes—treason, premeditated murder—have usually been considered capital crimes. These are serious crimes, punishable by long sentences, or execution. *Capital punishment*—death—is rarely used in the United States anymore; Gary Gilmore, the Utah murderer, shot by a firing squad in 1977 was the first such victim in this country since 1967.

The classifications of misdemeanor and felony and the

laws regulating arrest, bail, trial, and sentencing are written to apply equally to all. But do they?

Certainly most policemen or judges—or any of the administrators and technicians—in the American system mean well. Yet most criminologists agree that each step of the way involves important kinds of discrimination.

Let us consider the policeman who took Tina down to headquarters for questioning.

The policeman is our basic weapon against crime. But while he may help catch a burglar or mugger, there are some criminals against whom he has no weapons at all. They fall under the heading of "white-collar criminals." These are the business criminals, and, instead of holding up gas stations for $64, they rob in more skillful ways and for bigger stakes. The white-collar criminal, wrote criminologist Edwin Sutherland 25 years ago, has "respectability and high social status . . . ," and commits crimes ". . . in the course of his occupation."

A typical white-collar crime is price fixing. Executives from a number of different stores meet secretly. They know that if only Store X raises its prices the public will go to Stores Y and Z. If all three raise prices at the same time, the consumer will have no choice. So the next day all three stores have products selling at higher prices.

The U.S. Chamber of Commerce says that this kind of white-collar crime amounts to $40 billion per year, 200 times the amount taken by all the bank robbers in the country.

White-collar crimes include embezzling or bribery and many kinds of fraud which are difficult to detect. Let's say an insurance adjuster examines a claim and finds damage worth $300.

"I'll put it down as $1,200," he tells the claimant. Then you give me $300."

Most police arrests come about because there has been a complaint. But who is going to complain here?

White-collar criminals are often subtle about the way they

The arrest sets the wheels of our justice system in motion.

propose breaking the law. One of the authors had a friend who had been hired by the state to investigate the advertising claims of land developers. After inspecting one site, he was taken aside by the developer.

"I'd like to send you around to look at my other office," the developer said. "Give you an insight into how we run things."

"Fine. Where is it?"

"Paris."

"I couldn't report him if I wanted to," the friend said later. "But he could have flown me to Paris, wined and dined me, and never mentioned the word *bribe*. I would have gotten the message."

How are the police to investigate these crimes effectively? Yet, according to a September 1975 *New Times* article, while robberies increased by 12% from 1968 to 1974, white-collar crime rose by 313%.

Other criminal groups usually find ways to avoid serving time. These are the large, tightly run criminal operations whose control extends through gambling, prostitution, smuggling, and drug traffic. To distinguish them from the solo efforts of a bank robber or embezzler, police refer to this type of lawbreaking as "organized crime." They are to the freelance criminal what supermarkets are to the corner grocery store. And the most highly publicized is what on TV is often called "the Mafia."

This is not a new development.

"Organized criminal gangs," according to a 1951 report of Senator Estes Kefauver's Special Committee to Investigate Organized Crime in Interstate Commerce, "are firmly entrenched in our large cities in . . . gambling as well as . . . narcotics and commercialized prostitution . . . labor and business, racketeering, black marketing, etc.

". . . Despite known arrest records, the leading hoodlums in the country remain for the most part immune from prosecution and punishment [through] what is popularly known as the 'fix.' "

The situation isn't any different today. In fact, some authorities estimate that profits from the wide assortment of organized illegal activities total about $20 billion each year.

"In many suburban areas of the nation," Fred J. Cook wrote in his book *Mafia!,* "it is impossible to get garbage collected or to build a new schoolhouse without dealing at exorbitant prices with Mafia controlled firms. Through their huge bankrolls and menacing power, these Mafia-held firms have driven out all honest competition."

That isn't to say the police aren't kept busy. The trouble is that fully 40% of the people they arrest have committed crimes which some say shouldn't result in punishment at all.

These are the "crimes without victims." At least physically they have injured neither people nor property. These are criminals: the boy caught with an ounce of marijuana in his car; the prostitute who agrees to have intercourse with a man for $20; a run-away child; a drunk.

Police vice squads, for example, often spend their time posing as customers. A cop, dressed in street clothes, will approach a suspected prostitute on the street. He allows her to proposition him. After she has taken the money, he flashes his badge and makes the arrest.

It is too simple to say that no one is hurt by prostitution. Even those who argue that sexual habits are an individual matter agree that prostitution often leads to violent crimes. The customer may be robbed—or the prostitute beaten by his or her pimp. Yet, the amount of time devoted to vice arrests—or for drunkenness and the other offenses which are called victimless—is enormous.

In fact, about a third of all arrests in the United States are for public drunkenness at the expense of at least $100 million annually. Drug laws also eat up manpower and money. Edwin Schnur, in an essay on victimless crime, cites a California study which estimated that in 1968 "California alone spent some $72 million to enforce its laws against marijuana."

So there are problems facing the police which are not of their making. They would exist if every cop were a model of efficiency and honesty. And like the rest of us, they are not. Recently, the President's Crime Commission decided to look into police honesty. One professor gathered 36 observers. They each accompanied policemen for 49 straight days. They traveled in patrol cars. They watched booking procedures in high-crime precincts in Boston, Chicago, and Washington, D.C.

The police knew they were objects of a study. Even so, the observers saw one out of every five break the law. Policemen stole from drunks. They took bribes in both cash and merchandise. In return, they tore up speeding tickets or even changed their testimony in court.

Observers reported 37 unprovoked attacks on citizens.

Similar reports have been made elsewhere; a highly publicized one came from the 1971 Knapp Commission Investigation of the New York City Police. The commission reported that the police were involved in illegal drug activity. In Harlem, the average take from addicts and pushers by one crime-prevention squad was $1,500 a month. And it flatly stated that almost all units responsible for enforcing gambling laws got payoffs from gamblers.

Many policemen show racial prejudice. The report of the presidential commission found an overwhelming prejudice against black people—72% of all policemen believed blacks are more likely than whites to commit crimes.

Police patrol black neighborhoods more frequently than white. They have a tendency to pick up more blacks than whites. For years, black leaders protested the "stop and frisk" techniques used in ghetto areas. They argued that police frisked innocent people in black areas but never in suburbs a few miles away.

Often, police are easier on white offenders. Jessica Mitford relates the story of some high school seniors in Piedmont, a wealthy California town, who decided to have some fun. They ran through town, committing the following crimes: arson, breaking and entering, assault, car theft, and rape.

The police knew who the kids were. They were the children of executives, businessmen, and politicians. Afterward, they got together with the parents and their lawyers and held a conference. "We'll discipline these kids," the parents promised. No arrests were made.

It is a procedure often followed by police in wealthy areas. For the identical crimes, the poor or black child might be arrested, imprisoned in a juvenile detention home, and aimed by a juvenile court judge toward prison.

And once the suspect is arrested and enters our court system, he finds that if he has little or no money, his troubles have just begun. In 1970, nearly 100,000 people spent time behind bars because they couldn't afford a fine averaging $100.

Poor people cannot afford lawyers who will defend them

vigorously at all stages. Private lawyers are expensive. Instead, the poor must often use court-appointed counsel. Usually, their lawyer is a *public defender*—a man hired by the state or federal government to defend those too poor to pay. Public defenders may be inexperienced, but usually their problem is simply a heavy caseload which makes it impossible to spend much time on any one client. Not surprisingly, figures show that those with court-appointed lawyers get sentenced nearly twice as severely as those who hire their own lawyers.

Another problem is *bail,* the money an accused person deposits with the court in order to win temporary release until trial. Poor people often cannot afford it. Yet, whether or not an arrested person can post bail may be directly related to whether or not he or she will be found guilty: one Rand Institute study in New York City showed that prisoners who are out on bail before their trial are found guilty less often than those who stay in jail. In any case, the system of posting bail means that the amount of money you have determines whether you stay behind bars or walk the streets.

Like the poor, blacks are less likely to secure bail after an arrest. They are more likely to be indicted and less likely to have their cases dismissed.

Just as the background of the policeman affects the arrest, so do the background and prejudices of the judge affect the sentence. In Florida, for example, judges can place a guilty person on probation without placing "guilty" on his record. Recently, three social scientists studied 2,419 of those decisions. When they compared similar cases, they found that 40 to 60% more blacks than whites were sent out with "guilty" labels.

Other studies agree. Judges, looking at similar cases, find blacks guilty more often than whites—in Connecticut, one study examined 100,000 guilty findings. It saw blacks found guilty eight times more than the whites and sent to prison ten times more often.

Green Haven State Prison; New York.

There are other disturbing aspects to our judicial system. In the big American cities, many suspects who are completely innocent may wait for years to come to trial and be cleared. In Chicago, an average of 448 days go by before an arrested man or woman accused of a felony has the case resolved.

The American court is like a tiny funnel trying to handle hundreds of gallons of water at once. It backs up, spills over, and does only part of the job. In Manhattan, in 1974, the District Attorney's Office felt it had good cases against 326 murder suspects. But for Assistant District Attorney Frank Keenan, this wasn't much consolation.

"We would never be able to try everybody," he said to a reporter writing for *New York* magazine. "It is just physically impossible."

"What's the maximum number of killers you could possibly try in a year?"

"About 40."

A year later, Keenan proved himself fairly accurate. Manhattan's Homicide Bureau had tried 46 killers out of 326.

The solution for the courts especially in our large cities is called *plea bargaining*. After negotiation between the defense attorney and the prosecutor, the accused forgoes a jury trial and agrees to plead guilty to a lesser crime than the one he has been charged with in return for a lighter sentence. By pleading guilty, he avoids a lengthy trial and the courts can dispose of more cases. And here is a startling fact: while most Americans imagine that criminals are sent to jail after a jury trial, jury trials are unusual. "Between 75 to 90% of all felony convictions," writes criminologist Robert Sommer, "are obtained as a result of plea bargaining."

Sing Sing; New York.

A well-known example involved former Vice-President Spiro Agnew. U.S. Attorney James R. Thompson, now Governor of Illinois, who worked on the Agnew case said, "I've never seen a stronger case of bribery and extortion. If it had gone to trial, I'm sure he would have been sent to jail. He was simply a crook." Agnew's lawyer bargained for a lesser charge, arguing that Agnew did not want the nation to get into a "lengthy, bloody and convulsive battle." Former Attorney General Elliot Richardson also fought to keep Agnew from going to jail. The result: Agnew was allowed to plead guilty to one charge of federal income tax evasion. His sentence was a $10,000 fine, three years probation—and no jail sentence.

Plea bargaining does more than benefit the guilty. It can hurt the innocent.

Two days before Christmas Day, 1973, two college students watched a speeding Thunderbird crash into a limousine on New York's 80th Street. Two people were killed and seven injured though the students didn't know it then. They did see the driver jump from the Thunderbird, though, and run away. They saw a drunken man sitting in the passenger seat. They reported it to the District Attorney.

But the drunk, a man named Lee Johnson, was charged with two counts of murder and ten felonies. He stayed in jail for 14 months. The reason? The D.A. was offering 18 to 20 years in prison, while Johnson's lawyer, ignorant of the student testimony, felt forced to negotiate. The negotiating born out of the plea bargaining system kept the innocent Johnson in jail for over a year until he was acquitted.

The caseload faced by most courts is impossible to handle any other way than by plea bargaining. In 1970, in New York City, only 552 out of 94,042 arrests for felonies came to trial.

Plea bargaining, though, does not guarantee justice. In a typical plea bargaining case, the prosecutor throws serious charges at the accused, even if he can't possibly prove them.

He threatens the alleged offender, who may already have been in jail for months, with long years in prison.

It is a threat he can usually make good. Chances for conviction are high in a trial. Of all the cases in federal district courts that went to trial by jury in 1971, 72.9% ended in convictions. This is an incentive for the defendent to negotiate.

In addition, sentences handed down by a jury are generally more severe than if the defendant had plea bargained. The Administrative Office of the United States District Courts found that in federal court jury trials, defendants found guilty got sentences that were three times more severe than those pleading guilty at arraignment.

Stanton Bloom, formerly of the Cook County Public Defender's Office, says, "That's the penalty imposed for taking up the court's time."

So, when the suspect gets the offer, he may be wise to plead guilty to lesser charges—even if he is innocent.

Judges say that if plea bargaining were eliminated and every accused man were given a jury trial, the criminal courts would be so overcrowded that they would grind to a halt. Perhaps. But jury trials do not guarantee justice either.

The expensive, private criminal lawyer is knowledgeable about packing the jury box—that is, selecting sympathetic jurors. He has the time and staff to research his case. In fact, there are research firms which specialize in surveying a town to determine what attitudes local jurors are likely to have. (Do they dislike long hair? Or aggressive women?) These are resources denied the public defender.

Finally, after the verdict is in, comes the sentence. Here, too, justice is imperfect.

Laws differ in different states. The minimum sentence for armed robbery is one year in ten of the states, five years in 12 states, and death in two states. Someone arrested for incest in California could, in theory, get 50 years in prison. In Virginia,

he would be a misdemeanant with no more than one year behind bars.

Sentences even vary within states. The Federal Bureau of
Prisons reports that a man found guilty of stealing a car in
Brooklyn gets an average sentence of 51 months. Across the
East River, in Manhattan, he'd get an average sentence of only
30.7 months.

Then—and more difficult to pinpoint—there are the differences in sentences between blacks and whites. Not only are
more blacks arrested, tried, and found guilty than whites, but
they also stay longer in prison.

Generally, convicted blacks get longer sentences than
whites. They are offered fewer paroles. Between 1930 and
1966, when the death penalty was fashionable, over half of the
3,857 people legally killed were black, even though blacks
made up only 10% of the population.

Does this simply mean that blacks commit terrible crimes?
As one study in Florida made clear, the answer is no. Between
1940 and 1964 in that state, 285 men were found guilty of
rape. Fewer than 5% of the 133 whites but 35% of the 152
black men were executed.

Sentencing also discriminates against the poor—for example, when judges offer the choice of paying a fine or going
to jail.

An indeterminate sentence means that instead of getting
five years in prison, the criminal will get from "two to seven"
years. Even a flat sentence of five years, though, carries with it
a form of indeterminate sentencing. Prisoners can earn a reduction of their sentence by behaving well—that is, the way
the prison officials want. The officials, in turn, naturally, can
take away "good time" if they think a prisoner has been misbehaving.

In the federal system, a prisoner serving a flat sentence is
eligible for parole after serving a third of his sentence. So, a
six-year term is really a "two to six." There is much talk and

Lock-up. Dwight Correctional Center; Illinois.

some action in state legislatures around the country, therefore, toward eliminating the indeterminate sentence.

As we have seen, indeterminate sentencing became popular with the new drive to rehabilitate prisoners in the 1870's. Now most states use it. The legislatures have set up maximum and minimum times for each crime. The judge, instead of picking a fixed number of years, sends the convict to prison for "the term prescribed by law."

In the hands of some prison officials, the indeterminate sentence becomes a weapon. Prisoners are told, "You better do as we say if you want to make parole." Sometimes such threats are used to keep prisoners from appealing cases or writing letters to editors.

Often, a prisoner doesn't make parole even if he has been a pretty good prisoner. Prisoners have been denied parole for trying to organize a prisoner's union, even for swearing.

There is some evidence that the indeterminate sentence has resulted in longer sentences. Judges, afraid of letting criminals out too early, will sentence a criminal not to two years, for example, but to two to five. The prisoner is then in for the maximum with the burden on him to prove he should get out earlier.

Jessica Mitford cites a study at Indiana State Prison made when the indeterminate sentence began to be used. Men given indeterminate sentences in 1900 served an average of 6 months and 23 days longer than men committing the same crimes in 1890 who had been given flat sentences. By 1906 the time difference had stretched to more than a year.

Arrest. Trial. Sentencing. How well do they serve the ends of justice?

It is possible in looking at the problems of our criminal justice system to forget the good points.

Policemen, for example, serve vital functions.

The popular image of the policeman is that of the crime solver, a real-life Starsky or Hutch, spotting a burglar from the patrol car, then reaching for the siren and flooring the accelerator as the burglar darts down some garbage can-lined alley.

Actually, that rarely happens. One Los Angeles survey concluded that a patrolman in that city would detect a burglary every three months and a robbery every 14 years.

But patrolmen *are* important to people who are lost, to drivers in bottle-necked traffic, to runaways, to people who have been hit by cars, and to someone having a heart attack on the sidewalk.

They can also prevent crime. New Yorkers, frightened by what appeared to be a huge increase in subway crime, found this out in 1979. In fact, it isn't clear that there was such an increase. But when New York's Mayor Koch temporarily doubled the number of cops on subway patrol, complaints during peak hours fell by more than half.

Similarly, judges and prosecutors perform valuable services. The best case for this comes from Charles Silberman, a man who can extend compassion even to judges. He writes that "a seemingly irrational and unjust adult judicial process produces results that are surprisingly just." Silberman points out, for example, that the sentencing disparities criticized so often may be the result of differing values in each community.

Let us keep that in mind as we turn to the next step for the convicted lawbreaker: life inside prison.

Tina was one of those who was unlucky enough to get caught. She had yet to set foot inside a prison. But she had already heard some stories about prison life.

"I heard that they shave all your hair off, you had to wear stripes and a bunch of bad things," she said when we talked with her. "And they hung women in the basement and they beat us every day and you were fed slop."

It turned out that these fears were unfounded—mostly. But despite all the problems of the judicial system so far, the worst began for Tina only when she stepped inside the gates at Dwight.

In the next chapter, we will take a close look at what life is like for her and other men and women serving sentences in the modern American prison.

7

Inside

Whether you come from north or south, the drive to the Dwight Correctional Center is pleasant. In 1931, the year the prison was built, it was quite a trip to cover the 80 miles of rural blacktop separating Dwight from downtown Chicago. Today, on Route 55, it takes little over an hour.

But even now there are rolling cornfields and green soybean fields almost within sight of the brown brick walls. Sometimes the guards stop at roadside stands and pick up melons and sweet corn on the way home.

When Tina rode through the gates of Dwight, she entered one of the better prisons in the United States. Life there, like life in many women's prisons, is not outwardly violent or brutal. Its warden at the time Tina arrived was a young Ph.D. candidate in criminology, determined to avoid the abuses of the past.

Dwight is a prison where most of the measures called for by those reformers in Cincinnati in 1870 have taken effect. There is psychological testing, individualized treatment, classes, and a work program. If the prison system succeeds at all, it should succeed at Dwight.

When she entered Dwight, Tina was assigned, not to a cell block, but to a "cottage." Her cell—furnished with a stuffed mattress, warm blanket, bedspread and matching curtains, and even a radio—was a far cry from the cold floors and moldy straw beds of John Howard's time. Most nutritionists would find Tina's typical prison lunch of hotdogs on a bun, lettuce salad, and potato chips a little on the starchy side; still it is far more balanced and healthful than prison meals of even 50 years ago.

One thing that has not changed very much in prison life is the regimented routine. But, at Dwight, there is some flexibility within that routine. Although residents in maximum security were locked in their cells at 8:30, Tina, like others in minimum and medium security, could stay up until 2:00 A.M. After that, she was required to stay in her cell.

Every morning at six, a correctional officer strode down her cottage hall and knocked on the door to wake Tina up.

Dwight Correctional Center; Illinois.

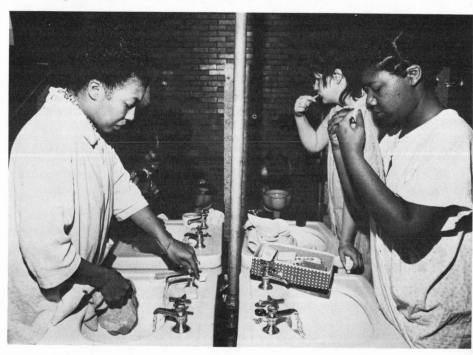

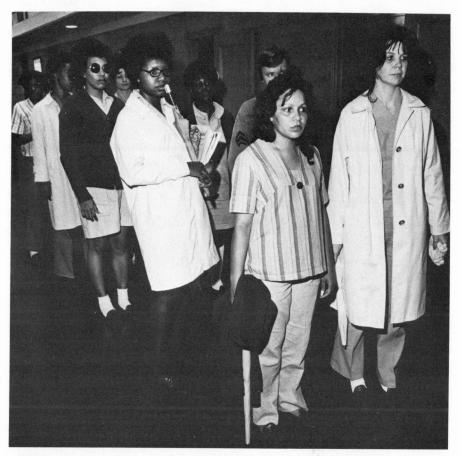

Morning whistle count, Dwight Correctional Center; Illinois.

Tina then brushed her teeth, took the quick sponge bath she was allowed, made her bed, and helped sweep the hallway.

The cottages themselves were locked until exactly 6:55 A.M., when Tina and the other 21 cottage inmates marched two by two to the dining hall for breakfast. About 40 minutes later, a whistle blew—the signal for the inmates to stand, a few at a time, deposit their silverware in trays, and go to work. Again regulated by whistles, the prisoners returned for lunch at 11 o'clock, then worked until 3:45 when they ate dinner.

"Free time" followed, slightly misnamed because it was only as free as their guards chose to make it. Some correctional officers, wanting their own free time or believing that inmates should be punished, locked the women in their cells where they could read or sleep. Other officers, believing that the inmates should have some freedom of movement in the cottages, let the inmates shower or talk with other inmates.

Between six and eight, Tina could choose between staying in the cottage, attending a special program or an exercise class, or going to recreation—softball in the summer or roller skating in the winter.

Based on Tina's experience, we might conclude that boredom is the worst aspect of present-day prison life. But if we look deeper—into conditions at Dwight as well as in the 200 or so other state and federal prisons in America—we find many other problems.

Oddly enough, Dwight's rural setting, which seems so pleasant to visitors, may be one of its biggest drawbacks. In the nineteenth century, locating prisons in the countryside made some sense; the prisoners could operate a farm and raise enough food to feed the entire prison population. Besides, most of the inmates came from rural areas. When the American population, and the heaviest concentrations of crime, began to shift toward urban areas, you might expect that prisons would have moved closer to the cities as well. But this did not happen. As late as 1971, all 23 of the newest American prisons had been built in rural areas.

There are a number of reasons for this. Citizen lobbies often oppose plans to build prisons in heavily populated neighborhoods. Urban prisons are also much more expensive to build and to staff; everything costs more in the city, from the land for a large structure like a prison to the guards' salaries.

In addition, many people believe that country living is clean living. The theory is that sending convicts to the country removes them from bad influences and puts them into an environment where they can develop new habits.

The truth, though, is that rural prisons tend to separate convicts from their families and communities. Visiting an inmate who is confined in a rural prison creates a hardship for many families, especially those who do not own cars. Also, many groups that might do volunteer work with prisoners, and many trained professionals who might be interested in working with prisoners, never do so at all because the prisons are so isolated.

Politics also plays a part in the selection of prison location. Many state legislatures used to be under the control of rural politicians who saw prisons as profitable industries for their districts. A state representative could be sure that the prison officials would have to buy supplies from businesses in his area. And he could reward people who had helped in his campaign by getting them hired as prison wardens, guards, and cooks.

This type of political hiring, known as patronage, still goes on today—even when the wardens are Ph.D.'s. It is a system with unfortunate consequences: it is hard to find the best guards possible when the most important item on their job application is whether they are Democrat or Republican.

Hiring prison employees from the vicinity of the rural prison means there will be a cultural gap between guards and prisoners. Often, there is a racial gap as well. In Attica, before the riot, over 60% of the inmates were black or Puerto Rican, and 77% came from urban areas. But the majority of the staff came from rural areas—and it was entirely white except for one black teacher and one Puerto Rican corrections officer.

The racism a black suspect meets upon his arrest and trial continues in prison. In many institutions, job assignments are made on the basis of color. Blacks are also selected less often for furlough or work-release programs.

A minor incident that occurred at Dwight shows how cultural differences can create tension between inmates and guards. There, most of the inmates were urban. Many were black. They found it hard to communicate with the largely white, rural staff. Language they considered quite ordinary could get them into trouble. One day, at work in the laundry, an inmate used the word "broad."

"We don't use that word," a supervisor said.

A little later, the inmate was overheard using the word "dude."

"We don't use that word *either*," said the supervisor.

The hostility guards feel toward inmates sometimes escalates into extreme brutality. Not too long ago, in Louisiana, seven women prisoners claimed they were punished by being beaten, stripped to their underwear, and handcuffed together in two cells. Then guards gassed them with a spray which burned their eyes and made it hard to breathe.

In Soledad Prison in California, one inmate wrote of some punishments aimed directly at rebellious black inmates.

> The prison official here stopped serving meals and deliberately selected the Caucasian and Mexican inmates to serve the meals and they immediately proceeded to poison our meals . . . with cleansing powder, crushed glass, spit, urine and feces while the officials stood by.

In 1970, black legislators investigating conditions inside the maximum security cells at Soledad concluded, "If even a small fraction of the reports received are accurate, the inmate's charges amount to a strong indictment of the prison's employees on all levels as cruel, vindictive, dangerous men."

These incidents are extreme, but beatings and other tortures imposed by guards still go on in many prisons. The psychology department of the University of Rhode Island recently conducted a study to measure the "violence potential" of inmates and correctional officers. This study found that the two groups were "almost identical"—but that the inmates were slightly *less* violent. Dr. Allen Berman, the tester, said the results showed that the officers had "the potential for even more unexplained lashing out" than the inmates.

What makes prison guards so prone to violence?

Some psychologists suggest the work attracts people who want to dominate and control. On the other hand, the job itself may create pressures that lead to violence.

David Fogel, who was Director of the Illinois Law Enforcement Commission, is one of the few writers on prison problems to have some sympathy for the guards. Their job is hard and unrewarding, he points out. Guards are surrounded by people who hate them, people who, in the past, have murdered, robbed, and assaulted even those they didn't hate. "Guards," says Fogel, "watch inmates become certified mechanics, high school graduates, and even college graduates. . . . The convicts are the recipients of much expensive attention." Meanwhile, the guards receive low pay and little respect from society as a whole. "There is little cultural pride attached to being a prison guard."

Fogel suggests that the guard's job was actually easier in the old days. Then he was issued a whip. Preventing escapes and keeping order was the extent of his responsibility. Today, he is still told to keep order—but without violating the edicts of a battery of sociologists, lawyers, and teachers.

San Quentin; California.

But guards still have methods of keeping order, and in the name of discipline, they can be brutal. The most widespread method of punishment goes by several names: prison officials call it "segregation," "isolation," or "solitary confinement." Prisoners call it "the hole."

A wide variety of offenses can send a prisoner into solitary confinement. Treating the staff with disrespect. Disobedience. Quarreling. Fighting. Swearing. Wearing dirty clothing. Being late for a meal or for work. These are all violations for which offenders have been punished by solitary confinement.

Periodically, inmates end up in the hole for more unusual reasons. An inmate at a Pennsylvania prison once decided she was tired of taking a shower standing on a bare concrete floor. Inmates had some freedom of movement at her institution, so she was able to sneak into an administrator's room. While a friend stood guard, she filled the tub with water and bubble bath and crawled in.

"The girl who was my lookout fell asleep," she later recalled. "The next thing I knew, Miss Taylor came up, opened the door and asked me, 'What do you think you're doing?' 'What the hell does it look like I'm doing? I'm taking a bath.'" the inmate replied.

Few would argue that she should have gone undisciplined. But for this incident, the inmate received four months in solitary.

Conditions in the hole vary. Generally, they are barren rooms where there is nothing to do or to read. Some prisons have mattresses on the floor. Some have blankets and sheets. Others do not. Some have single light bulbs in exposed sockets which the inmates cannot turn on or off. Some have toilets. Inmates are sometimes given a Bible, just as they were in the Walnut Street Jail centuries ago. Sometimes, inmates can have other books.

Dwight Correctional Center; Illinois.

Psychologists warn that isolating prisoners can lead to insanity. "I could no longer be responsible for these patients," one prison psychologist said. "These are exactly the conditions to drive a man further into psychosis." In spite of such criticisms, solitary confinement continues to be used because wardens and guards consider it necessary.

Psychologists, sociologists, and medical personnel are supposed to play an important role in reforming prisoners, but in reality, they and other rehabilitative personnel make up only 7% of the 120,000 men and women being paid to run prisons in the United States. Custody, not rehabilitation, is still the first concern of prison officials.

Some prisons do have up-to-date, well-equipped hospitals. But too often, sick calls are run in assembly line fashion. Often, doctors don't examine the patients. The Dwight physician remarked, "These girls aren't sick. I see them week after week, and they always have the same complaint. All they need is a sugar pill."

Recently, another area of prison medical treatment has come under attack: medical testing. Anyone can volunteer for medical research. But these tests are often painful and dangerous, so most of us pass up the experience. In prison, there are many pressures to volunteer for such tests. National pharmaceutical companies pay inmates to become research subjects; the pay is low, but usually more than prisoners can make at their regular jobs. And volunteering for these programs is looked on favorably by parole boards. Along with mental patients, prisoners make up almost the entire pool of subjects for the initial human testing of all new drugs in this country.

"Many prison doctors," one book argues, "have conducted invaluable pieces of research into medical problems, with prisoners volunteering." But the rights of prisoners have sometimes been abused. Early in 1974, newspapers reported that a group of inmates in a southern prison had advanced syphillis. An investigation turned up the fact that these inmates, who

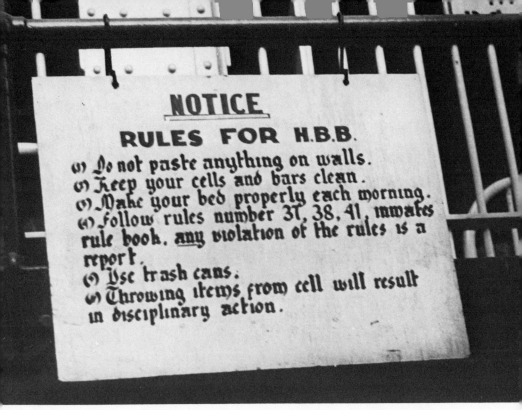

NOTICE

RULES FOR H.B.B.

(1) Do not paste anything on walls.
(2) Keep your cells and bars clean.
(3) Make your bed properly each morning.
(4) Follow rules number 31, 38, 41, inmates rule book. <u>any</u> violation of the rules is a report.
(5) Use trash cans.
(6) Throwing items from cell will result in disciplinary action.

Inmate photo.

hadn't understood the dangers, had been used as guinea pigs about 15 years before in an experiment that involved injecting them with syphillis bacteria. Some inmates had died. The rest had gone untreated. This exposé led to stricter laws governing the use of human beings for medical research, but the basic question remains unanswered: is it fair to use prisoners as guinea pigs?

What about counseling and testing intended to help the prisoners themselves? In the last decade or so, more and more prisons have recognized the need for such services. A few years ago, there were only 12 states which had psychologists, psychiatrists, or social workers in any prison. Now, nearly all states have all three.

But look what happens:

When Tina entered Dwight, she was interviewed by a social worker. The social worker decided Tina would be happiest working in the sewing room. Her suggestion was ignored.

"I feel useless here," she said later. "I tell the staff what Tina needs. But nobody listens. If prison industry has an opening, they get the next available inmate. If the kitchen needs somebody, they get the next person. It's all based on economy."

Inmates find it hard to trust prison staff. When Tina came to Dwight, the only staff psychologist was also the staff disciplinarian. "Hell," one Dwight inmate said, "We won't talk to her . . . You tell her your problem and she slaps you with a ticket and you go to the hole. Now, how's she gonna help me that way?"

In 1958, Alfred Schnur made fun of the "new penology" in an article published in the *Journal of Criminal Law*. His study found a ratio of 23 full-time psychiatrists to 161,587 prisoners. "Each psychiatrist," concluded Schnur, "is responsible for 7,026 inmates . . . there is not more than 82 seconds of psychiatric help available for each inmate during a whole month." These statistics would be somewhat better today, but in many prisons psychiatric services still exist in name only.

Social and psychiatric help is part of the new approach to rehabilitation, but job training and education is still the mainstay of such efforts. Since the idea of training prisoners to do useful work has been around for a long time, we might expect these programs to be successful. But are they?

Tina's daily routine was designed to rehabilitate her. In fact, when she entered Dwight, Tina became eligible for certain free vocational and educational programs that she would have had no access to if she were not a convicted criminal. The irony of this situation is not lost on prison critics. Newspaper stories about criminals who receive college degrees behind bars sometimes create the impression that prisons have become "country clubs" and that prisoners are being given opportunities not open to the general public.

Correctional officers at Dwight like to stress the educational side of prison life. "Our inmates can learn any number of skills," said one proudly. And another, interviewed while she was walking down the cottage hall, locking cell doors, added, "We do the best we can with what we have . . . They lead an organized life. They are provided with an opportunity to further their education."

Yet Tina, as she joined her fellow inmates to put in a day's work at the greenhouse, was far from optimistic: "I have to water the plants," she said, "and then plant new ones. All day. Oh, and sometimes I make flower arrangements for the superintendent. And I transplant some . . . That's not gonna do me much good."

Some of Tina's friends at Dwight did have skilled jobs. One was a typist at the prison infirmary. Another prisoner helped run the kitchen, and another was a supervisor in the prison laundry.

Only a handful of inmates get challenging jobs, however, because there simply aren't enough to go around. Most jobs don't train prisoners for the future; they simply keep the prison running: inmates take out the garbage, sweep, carry hot water

Dwight Correctional Center; Illinois.

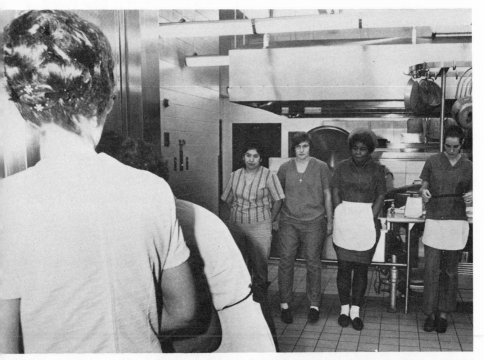

to the cells, sew prison clothing, and do laundry. Since inmates do not receive real wages or have any practical incentive to do their jobs well, it is doubtful whether these assignments even teach good work habits.

Prison industry, once the great hope of rehabilitation advocates, has problems of its own. Ever since the depression, there has been opposition to prison manufacturing that competes with regular businesses. There is some justice in this argument: prison industries pay their workers between 5¢ and 25¢ an hour, with no sick days or fringe benefits. In 1971, they had a profit above sales of 17%—almost four times that of the rest of American industry. To keep from threatening the jobs of workers on the outside, most prison workshops now manufacture items like license plates that are not produced by private industry. But how can an inmate trained to paint numbers on license plates hope to get a similar job when he leaves the institution? He can't, and he is likely to resent hearing his work described as rehabilitation.

Vocational training programs that try to teach more useful skills often turn out to be just as irrelevant. Equipment may be old and obsolete: as late as 1951, San Quentin operated a jute mill. According to theory, prisoners would be able to get jobs in the jute industry after their release. Yet the nearest commercial jute mill was located in Holland. In another midwestern prison, cited by Sol Chaneles in his 1973 book *The Open Prison,* 1,000 inmates were enrolled in a training program that operated with one electrical motor, designed in 1914 and donated to the prison in 1922.

Even with excellent teaching equipment it would be difficult for prison administrators to predict what the labor market will be like by the time an inmate is freed. "You've got to have some sympathy for the people planning these programs," says one New York-based lawyer who works closely with them. "They have to decide what skills will be in demand 10, 15 years into the future. That's hard to do."

So, in spite of the emphasis on job training as a means of helping prisoners, the results have been disappointing. One follow-up study was conducted at Washington State Penitentiary, where inmates had been trained in such seemingly useful skills as office machine repair, auto mechanics, barbering, carpentry, and dry cleaning. Researchers concluded that inmates who had participated in these vocational training programs had *less* success staying on a job after release than those who did not take part.

The reasons this study turned out as it did are not clear, but other researchers have placed much of the blame on the inadequacy of the programs themselves. They fail to teach work habits, attitudes, and skills that are valuable after release. A 1969 report by the California Legislature's Assembly Office of Research criticized California prisons' industries for teaching skills that are "often antiquated" and called prison jobs "little better than idleness." The study concluded that the state's prison industries were "no more successful than other institutional busy-work programs." Statistics from other states seem to bear out these statements, especially since few prisoners get a chance to participate in these programs. For example, in 1980 only about 20% of New York State's 20,900 prisoners are enrolled in job-training programs.

Educational programs, ranging from basic reading and writing to college-level courses, seem to hold more promise for those prisoners who are interested in them. If Tina had chosen to do so, she could have taken secretarial courses instead of working in the greenhouse, or she could have attended classes to complete her high school education.

Today, more and more prisons are offering classes to inmates, but there is still no general policy for educating prisoners. Dwight had one full-time high school teacher, one part-time, elementary school teacher, and a full-time remedial reading teacher for about 150 inmates. Some textbooks were new, though many were old and outdated. In other prisons, courses are sometimes taught by the guards or by the inmates themselves.

In 1970, President Nixon's Task Force on Prisoner Rehabilitation reported that only 1% of the nation's prisoners were in educational programs and that less than half of 1% of the nation's total annual prison budget went for education. These figures broke down to about 60¢ per prisoner. All of these statistics would be larger today, but education still provides a goal for only a small minority of inmates.

Prisons rarely have good libraries, and this probably affects the typical prisoner much more than the lack of educational programs. We tend to think of convicts as semiliterate; in fact, inmates read *five times* as many books as the average citizen.

Federal prisons usually have trained librarians, but other institutions may not. Books may be old and worn out, and the selection is often limited to detective stories and religious tracts. Some prisons, though not all, allow inmates to receive approved books, magazines, and newspapers through the mail. There have been highly publicized cases of convicts—such as Caryl Chessman and Edgar Smith—who read voraciously in prison and transformed themselves into skilled writers. But there are still many prisoners who would take the opportunity to educate themselves through reading if they had access to a good library.

In spite of all the routines set up by guards, teachers, work supervisors, and social workers, the most important part of an inmate's prison experience is likely to be his or her relationship with other inmates. When Tina entered Dwight, she soon learned that inmates believe in loyalty to each other and not to the prison staff. She was told that when inmates stick together, it is a lot easier to do time.

Most of the brutality of prison life comes from the prisoners themselves. Inmates beat up and sometimes kill other inmates. This brutality is related to the prison cultural system. Inmates have their own rules—rules which differ from the ad-

Dwight Correctional Center; Illinois.

ministration's rules. In some prisons—usually not in women's—inmates judge and punish other prisoners for infrac-
tions of their rules.

"Good time" is what inmates call the time taken off their
sentences for good behavior. The inmates' drive to get and
maintain their good time aggravates the tension. Inmates feel
they cannot go to a guard for help if another inmate threatens
them. They fear that if the guard gets wind of a fight, the inmates involved might lose their good time. So they resolve
disputes among themselves. The weaker inmates end up bat-
tered. The strong have an easier time.

As important as the actual violence is the threat of violence. Inmates know that if they break an inmate rule, they
might be beaten up. They know that they can't go to a guard
for help. They know there's no way to escape the other inmates. And they know that the prison officials can do very little
to remedy the situation.

There is a kind of caste system or pecking order among inmates. The most important factor in the ranking procedure is
the crime committed. Mothers who kill their babies, for example are at the bottom of the scale. Those who have committed many crimes without getting caught, prior to conviction,
rank high. A bank robber or forger may rank high. Rapists
rank low.

If an inmate will do whatever is necessary for self-defense
and has friends to help him, he gets respect. Those reluctant to
fight back and those who have not lined up supporters rank
lower. The mentally retarded and physically weak rank low.

In addition, cleverness gets respect. Outside connections
get respect. Those who smuggle drugs and other illegal items
into the prison rank high. Those who abide by the inmates'
rules get respect.

Another inescapable part of prison life is homosexuality.
During the late 1940's, Alfred Kinsey studied the sex habits of
American men and women and reported that at least 35% of

prison inmates were involved in homosexual relations. In long-term institutions, no fewer than 60% were involved. In one institution, 90% participated.

At Dwight, homosexual relationships were the rule rather than the exception:

"You gonna tell me," one Dwight inmate said, a thumb thrust scornfully at her chest, "that you're gonna be locked up for eight years and not going to have something to do with another woman?"

Another inmate, sitting alone one night before going back to her cell, explained it a little more quietly:

"It's not forced. Women who would never get into that sort of thing on the street start looking up to some of the tougher women. Its comforting to find someone to sort of look out for you. You get to longing for affection—for some kind of meaningful relationship."

Most staffers at Dwight found this horrifying. They did their best to stamp out opportunities for homosexual contact. Inmates were forbidden to touch each other. They were forbidden even to fix each other's hair. Groups of inmates watching TV had to keep empty chairs between themselves and their neighbors. But these rules did little except to make the staff feel virtuous. Inmate lovers would ask others to post guard or keep the staff occupied with some distraction and send signals in case a guard approached. Some just took their chances and faced the consequences if they were caught.

Homosexuality exists in both male and female prisons. Often, relationships are based on friendship and even love, but many times, too, they involve coercion and violence. This is especially true in male prisons. Some prisoners become prostitutes for money. Younger and weaker prisoners may form a relationship with a more powerful inmate in exchange for protection. Inmates can threaten and sometimes force an unwilling partner to submit. Or, if all else fails, they resort to rape.

In Holmesburg, a male prison in Pennsylvania, inmates

willing to pay the guards were able to choose a sexual partner from among the prison population. The guards actually allowed informers—those who passed along secrets about other inmates—to pick other men to rape. Inmates who wouldn't go along took the chance of being beaten or put in solitary.

"You have three alternatives with rape. Submit, fight, or go over the fence," said one Missouri official to a prisoner. In that prison, it was common for other prisoners to have master keys to each cell. After being gang raped several times and after trying to fight his attackers, this convict was caught escaping. He argued that he was following instructions but the Missouri Supreme Court disagreed.

Whether the guards exploit the situation, as they did at Holmesburg, or try to eliminate it, as they did at Dwight, homosexuality is likely to remain a fact of prison life as long as inmates are isolated from members of the opposite sex. Some experts have suggested that the solution might be to permit frequent private overnight visits by the inmates' husbands and wives, and even boy friends and girl friends. Such visits are really not a new idea. Countries that were never influenced by reformist programs like the silent system have allowed such conjugal visits for years.

A few U.S. prisons have experimented, but for the most part, inmates can only meet with visitors in a large room where their conversations and behavior are observed by guards. Even this arrangement, a reform of the traditional practice of having inmates and guests separated by plexiglass dividers, is unpopular with many administrators who feel that it has now become much easier to smuggle drugs and other contraband into the prisons.

Prisons vary. One may be a 100-year-old building with high brick walls. Another might look like a college campus. One might have three men to a cell. The next might give each inmate a room to himself. Some prisons are plagued with bugs and rats. Others are not.

Some prisons let the inmates wear their own clothes in order to help them build up a sense of individuality. Others make the inmates wear striped, drab uniforms. Critics see this as one failure of the prison system. Why should a murderer in Rhode Island lead a prison life any different from a murderer in Connecticut?

But one thing is clear about all prisons in the United

States. From the first real attempt to change—at Walnut Street Jail in 1790—no prison has developed a program which clearly works to end crime.

This is true despite the staggering amount of money that goes into supporting the system. The figures are surprising. In 1970, the average cost of building one jail or prison cell was $12,000, and by 1980, it had risen to between $25–60,000. According to one estimate, between 1970 and 1980 about 10 million people passed through prisons at a total cost of over $30 billion.

Prison operating budgets double every ten years. It now costs between $7–$26,000 each year to house, clothe, and feed a single inmate. "We'd be better off," one prison official confessed, "closing the prisons and paying each prisoner to stay home."

"It's supposed to rehabilitate," one Dwight inmate said of the institution, "I been here three times and I don't know what's wrong with me because I haven't been rehabilitated yet."

Shortly before we left Dwight, we had one final talk with Tina. She summed up her feelings this way: "I know I committed a crime in society. If I have to pay for it the way they say— lock you up and do all they say—then O.K. . . . I'll do it cause I know I did wrong. But I was a mean little kid. I'm gonna be even tougher when I leave. A reformatory—that means a place to make you a better person. That's not here."

But what happens in prison is only part of the problem. In the next chapter, we will take a close look at the ex-con. We will see what happens to prisoners after they have passed through programs designed to rehabilitate and prepare them for a law-abiding life.

8

Getting Out

Ninety-nine percent of all prisoners eventually walk out.

It wasn't that way in the days of Henry VIII, when many waited in prisons until they were scheduled to hang. It wasn't that way aboard the English hulks where one-eighth of the prisoners died from disease or mistreatment. But in twentieth-century America, gaol fever is unknown and executions are rare.

Despite the flurry of legislation reinstituting capital punishment for some crimes, the chances are small that even a few of the hundreds of American prisoners presently on death rows around the country will be executed. Should the state have the right to take human life at all? The question is well worth discussion. But practically, it is a prospect few prisoners face. The great majority will someday be free to live and work alongside the rest of us.

Prisoners get out in four ways:

First, some have been wrongly convicted. Perhaps another person confesses to the crime or new evidence is uncovered. The prisoners then undergo a new trial or have their sentences reduced by the governor.

Some escape, most to be recaptured within minutes or days, but sometimes to avoid authorities for years. In 1933, a famous bank robber named Willie Sutton escaped from a New York prison. He led a quiet life for 17 years, until a crime magazine fan recognized him on the New York subway and pointed him out to police. It turned out Sutton had lived for years within one block of a police station.

A third way out is simply to serve the sentence. No matter how many rules he breaks or how many inmates he intimidates, a prisoner with a five-year sentence will be out within five years, unless he commits an actual crime within prison walls.

Finally, there is parole. Over 60% of adult felons in America are released on parole before reaching the maximum limit of their original sentences. The federal and state governments have parole boards which meet regularly at prisons to try to find the inmates who are already reformed and who can safely be released. Members of the boards review the criminal

Inmate photo, Riker's Island; New York.

records of every eligible inmate. They examine staff reports. They look at prison records. They interview the inmate personally. After release, a parolee periodically meets with a parole officer. When the term of parole has been served, the parolee receives a final discharge and is free.

It sounds good. The system pioneered by Captain Maconochie 125 years ago on Norfolk Island has made its mark on the American penal system. Yet those who have studied parole agree that the decision to release some prisoners while keeping others in confinement may have little rational basis.

A typical parole hearing may involve a ten-minute interview with the inmate. During that time period, the board members are expected to discover his emotional state and attitude. The staff reports, often written by counselors who are undertrained and overworked, may be distorted or sketchy. If the staff member has taken a dislike to the inmate, he may enter a negative report even if the inmate is perfectly well behaved. The parole board members will not know the difference.

Then the board member recites "parole granted" or "parole denied" into his dictaphone. Sometimes the reasons for the decision are explained to the inmate. Sometimes he is simply told there has been a "lack of progress." Inmates cannot appeal parole decisions as they can appeal the decision of a judge. This verdict is final.

What happens to a prisoner on parole?

The parolee signs a contract with the parole board. In exchange for his liberty he agrees to certain conditions. A typical parolee will agree not to leave his county—or even to move within the county—without permission of his parole officer. He agrees not to drive or buy a car. He will not drink alcoholic beverages or have sexual intercourse with anyone except his wife. And here is the catchall clause: he must "cooperate with his parole agent at all times."

The parole officer enforces these rules. He can search a parolee or the parolee's house at any time without a warning or warrant. The parolee can be arrested and jailed without bail—even if the officer only suspects he is violating one of the rules. The officer can recommend that parole be suspended. And it is a recommendation almost always followed by the parole board.

Some parole officers have degrees in social work. Others are former policemen or prison guards. Some are eager to help the parolee. Others see themselves as jailers. All of them have a dual role—they are supposed to act both as counselors and as guards, to represent the best interests of both the parolee and the prison. They also have enormous caseloads; most penologists estimate that 35 cases per officer is the highest load a parole officer can handle. But over two-thirds of parolees are in caseloads of over 100.

Recently, two sociologists studied the entire staff of a state parole agency. They showed each parole officer ten actual case histories where there were possible parole violations. The 316 officers were asked to decide whether the alleged violators should return to prison.

About half of the officers wanted to return six or seven to prison. But they did not agree on which to return. Five of the officers suggested that parole be revoked for all ten. One officer saw a violation in only one case.

It turned out the officers who had worked in prisons would revoke more paroles than those who had backgrounds in social work. Supervisors wanted fewer returns than parole agents.

In a second study, a University of Wisconsin professor asked ten trained parole officers and ten inexperienced people to look at 200 case studies of prisoners who had been paroled. About half of the 200 prisoners had been returned to prison. He wanted the two groups to predict who would break parole and who would not.

It turned out the laymen were able to predict more accurately than the parole officers. And the guesses of both groups were worse than a mere random sampling.

"Among adult offenders," write criminologists Norval Morris and Gordon Hawkins, "55 to 65 percent of those released are not subsequently returned. And only about one-third of those have been convicted of new felonies."

But early in 1974, a Citizens Inquiry on Parole and Criminal Justice reported that offenders released on parole return to prison in the same year only slightly less often than those who serve out their terms. That is, parolees don't do much better in the community than those who aren't paroled.

According to former Attorney General Ramsey Clark, 50% of those paroled in America either commit a new crime or violate parole rules. About 80% of these people end up back in prison.

What are we to conclude? That parole leaves wide room for abuse, that it has let out criminals who have committed the most brutal crimes and has kept in prison many who would lead productive lives if released, and that it is no picnic for the parolee.

Is parole useful? The verdict is still not in.

But whether a prisoner is paroled or returns to society after serving his or her full term, the adjustment can still be traumatic:

"They take a city girl," an inmate said, "and put her in prison and she picks tomatoes for four years. Then they send her back to the city as 'socially adjusted.' I was so adjusted that even the bus ride back to Philadelphia scared the hell out of me. The noise and the people talking and moving around. I just shut my eyes and prayed to survive the trip."

Her experience sounds a lot like a man just out of prison quoted in John Irwin's book *The Felon*. "The first time I started across the street, I remember, I was watching a car coming and I couldn't judge his speed very good. I couldn't tell if he was going to hit me or not. It was weird."

The woman from Philadelphia was lucky. She was returning home. One out of every ten inmates gets on that first bus or train with no idea where to go. Fifty thousand of the 100,000 long-term inmates who leave prison each year have no home to which they can return. Families have moved. Husbands or wives have divorced and remarried.

Some crime movies picture the ex-con walking out of prison and digging up the loot he had stashed away after his last bank job. In fact, few convicts have much money. Sometimes, the prison hands the ex-con $40 or $100 as he walks out of the gates, but that doesn't last more than a few days.

When ex-cons go job hunting, they find that they belong to a group with the highest rate of unemployment in America. Their rate is three to four times higher than that of the general working population. They often don't have salable job skills. And there is an even bigger barrier: discrimination. One study of 475 potential employers in many business fields, found that 311—almost two out of three—would not hire even qualified ex-cons and would fire them if they learned of their records after hiring.

Even the government discriminates. Said one ex-convict,

who applied to ten state departments for clerical work before being hired, "They said the state hires us, so I applied. I applied ten times. And on the application, they ask if you've ever been arrested for anything but a traffic violation. So I put down, *Yes*. It always happened. The interview was going good and then they'd seen I'd been arrested. Then they'd be real cool. One man sent me a letter. He said he wouldn't hire me on account of my *background*. One man asked about my work history. I told him I didn't work for six years because I was in prison. He cut the interview right then."

Nearly every state prohibits offenders from becoming doctors. If a doctor should be imprisoned, he can expect to lose his license to practice when released. Prisoners spend months learning how to be beauticians or barbers, only to find upon release that some states will not give anyone with a prison record the necessary license. Ex-convicts have a hard time getting real estate licenses. And there are barriers if they try to become veterinarians, embalmers, or accountants. In New York, ex-cons have been unable to get jobs as taxi drivers, longshoremen, or teachers.

The ex-con's problems don't end there. He might find that his possessions have been stolen or taken by a landlord or finance company. His children may have been placed in a foster home. He cannot get legitimate credit from lending companies or banks and may end up getting "street-corner" credit—and pay excessive rates. If he gets life or health insurance at all, he pays well above the average rates.

No laws prohibit people with prison records from moving into public housing projects. But many states have administrative policies that bar ex-convicts from good, low-cost housing. Nongovernmental landlords don't like to rent to them, either. They don't see them as trustworthy, responsible tenants.

No laws prohibit ex-convicts from going to high school, college, or vocational training centers. But some schools won't let them enroll.

In short, we tell the ex-convict, "You have paid for your crime in prison. Now you have another chance." We even pour money into job-training programs we hope will increase that chance. But we see to it that he has handicaps and restraints with every step he takes.

"Okay," some people argue. "Prison life is cruel. The ex-con has a tough time when he gets out. Most criminals never even see the inside of a prison. But doesn't prison rehabilitate some people? Doesn't it keep some really vicious people away from the rest of us? Doesn't it scare off some men and women who want to break the law?"

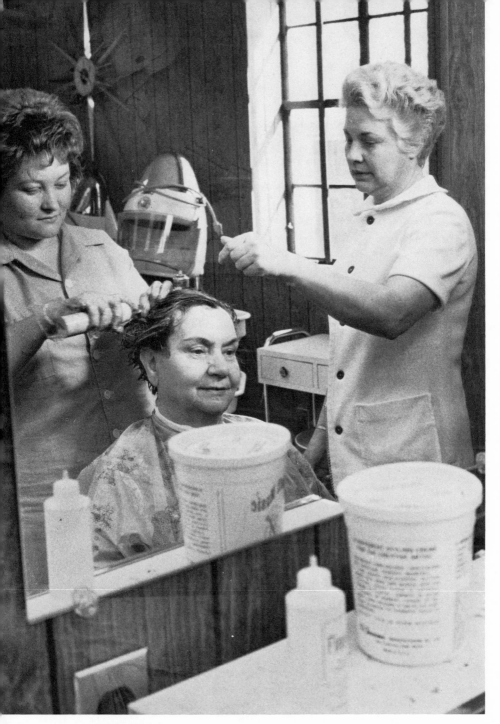

An inmate practices on a correctional officer at Dwight Correctional Center's beauty school.

The *recidivism rate*—the number of ex-cons who are caught breaking the law again—is one way of judging whether prisons rehabilitate.

The evidence is not clear cut; the figures vary. But even the lowest estimates of recidivism are disturbing: 40 to 80% of adult prisoners and 74 to 85% of juvenile offenders commit crimes after being released from prison. Ramsey Clark says 80% of all felonies are committed by repeaters. And more than half of all the people who leave prison return convicted of a serious crime.

What does the prison system in America accomplish? If there is anyone who has considered that question to exhaustion, it is penologist Robert Martinson. He was hired by the New York State Governor's Special Committee on Criminal Offenders specifically to answer the question "What works?"

For five years, Martinson worked on what eventually became a 1,400-page review of every scrap of research. In 1974, he wrote a 28-page summary of his findings.

Does a prison running "a truly rehabilitative program" turn out more successful individuals than a prison which merely leaves its inmates alone? What about programs going further than education or skill development? What about prisons that help with the deep problems prisoners face? What about prisons where the "inmate's whole environment is directed towards true correction" rather than towards custody or punishment? What about strictly medical treatment—drugs, for example? What influence does length of sentence have?

All were questions covered in Martinson's study. His conclusion: *"With few and isolated exceptions, the rehabilitative efforts that have been reported so far have had no appreciable effect on recidivism."*

And what about the deterrent effect of prison? "It is possible that there is indeed something that works," writes Martinson. But because so little research has been done in this area, "we know almost nothing about the 'deterrent effect.'"

We do know that crime simply *does not* decrease as penalties get tougher. For example; the FBI says that crime per every 100,000 people residing in the United States rose 35% between 1960 and 1965. Beginning in 1964, federal courts and most states judges began giving longer sentences. From 1964 to 1970 federal sentences became 38% longer.

But between 1965 and 1970—the harsher period—the national crime rate rose 45%.

Do rehabilitative programs work?

In Chapter One, we mentioned at least one study which seemed to indicate that the longer a man or woman stayed in prison the higher the chances were that he or she had of breaking the law again. That was the conclusion of one *American Bar Association* report: "If we, today, turned loose all of the inmates of our prisons without regard to the length of their sentences and, with some exceptions, without regard to their previous offenses, we might reduce the recidivism rate over what it would be if we kept each prisoner incarcerated until his sentence expired."

Studies do show that nearly all the violent criminals, upon release, commit new crimes which are far more violent than the ones which originally sent them to prison. Milton Luger, Director of the New York State Division of Youth said, "It would be better if young people who commit crimes got away with them because we just make them worse."

James Robinson of the National Council on Crime and Delinquency and Gerald Smith of the University of Utah made a thorough study of the different types of treatment in American prisons. They decided that putting a person in prison "will impair whatever potential he has for a crime-free future adjustment." Also, they decided, it made no difference what treatment was used in prison. What matters is incarceration, alone. The longer an inmate stays in prison, the more he will deteriorate and the more likely it is that he will recidivate. Perhaps that is why Norman Carlson, Director of the United States Bureau of Prisons, once commented, "Anyone not a criminal will be when he gets out of jail."

Then, should prisons be abolished? Our natural instinct is to say "Only if we *know* they don't work." But the more radical critics of corrections feel that isn't the point at all.

"You take a guy, and send him to prison because he's poor or black," said Dr. Jerome Miller, former Commissioner of Youth Services for the State of Massachusetts and Director of the Illinois Department of Children and Family Services. "You subject him to beatings. You make him obey ridiculous rules and regulations. You make him go without sex for years. You give him the most simpleminded and useless jobs to perform. You take away most of the basic rights of citizenship. Then you set him up so he finds it hard to get a job when he's out. Maybe you should have to prove to him that it's *going* to work."

We don't have to accept this statement in every detail to believe in the need to look at other ways than prison of dealing with lawbreakers.

9

What's Next

If you watch the men handling butcher knives and cleavers in the Peoria meat processing plant, they look very much alike. Dressed in work clothes and bloody smocks, they cut and package the meat which will go to 200 Pizza Huts all around the country.

But for one of them, a 35-year-old man named Arthur Baker, life is a little different. He is paid the same as the other men, but, every afternoon at 3:30, he hangs up his smock in the locker room reserved for cutters. He is met at the factory gate by a Department of Corrections counselor, and together they drive 20 miles to check back into the Peoria Community Correctional Center in Brimfield, Illinois.

During the day, Baker has been in touch with the center several times.

"It used to be different," he says. "But around a year ago some guys got caught smoking pot. So now when you leave, you got to check in every hour."

Baker doesn't like this. "They treat you like a kid," he says. Still, there is no doubt that this Center is unlike most prisons.

The Peoria Center is a *halfway house*. It's one kind of correctional institution becoming more popular in the United States. It houses convicts who, according to prison officials, are too well behaved to warrant imprisonment but whose crimes call for some sort of rehabilitative program.

Most prison reform proposals fall into one of three categories.

The first category is geared toward making life easier for inmates—to make prisons into what some call "sweet joints." The feeling of those who support these proposals is that the brutality of traditional "fortress prisons"—in 1974, there were 87 stabbings and 12 fatalities in San Quentin prison alone— fosters crime. They argue that it makes inmates more likely to repeat crimes and thus is itself a threat to society. They argue that to deprive lawbreakers of liberty is punishment enough, that we will accomplish more rehabilitation by treating convicts with dignity.

Among these proposals are:

—shorter sentences
—greater emphasis on prerelease programs
—smaller prisons
—urban locations
—better-qualified parole board members
—better living conditions, including improved food, medical
    treatment, visitation rights, and legal resources.

One such "sweet joint" is the Framingham, Massachusetts Correctional Institution. It is a coed minimum security prison and holds about 90 women and 60 men.

The women at Framingham, mostly in their early twenties, are in for crimes like prostitution or drug offenses. The men, in their twenties and thirties, have usually committed more serious crimes—murder or armed robbery. Most of them will be eligible for parole within a year to 18 months.

To those serving "hard time" in a more rigorously disciplined prison—and to some politicians—life at Framingham seems like a vacation. The inmates eat together, play cards together, and swim together in the outdoor pool which was built with proceeds from an annual Christmas fair. About half the inmates work in nearby cities. There are dinner dances and fashion shows.

Sex is out. But the inmates can hold hands. In fact, one inmate quoted in a *New York Times* article said, "That's the one thing that bugs me. If two women are together, the guards don't bother them. But if a man and a woman sit together on the grass for more than a few minutes, they break it up."

Another was more contented. "If you've got to be in prison, this is the place. I mean you wake up in the morning and you see trees and you walk down the walk with a chick. You can't beat it."

Not all examples of reform within prison walls come from the minimum security prisons. Washington State Penitentiary, in Walla Walla is a maximum security institution. Yet, in 1972, 1,200 convicts there took part in what *Life* magazine called "a radical experiment in prison reform." The inmates elected an Inmates Council, which had real power in deciding how the prison would be run.

The first election found "two killers, four holdup men, an arsonist and a rapist seated around the council table," according to *Life* reporter Barry Farrell. They were not pawns of the administration; in fact, early in the experiment, a resident was knifed. When the warden asked the council for help in finding the assailant, they turned him down.

Through the 1970's the experiments at Walla Walla have evoked enormous controversy. By now they involve far more than elections. Still, the Walla Walla experiments have been cited as an attempt to restore rights to inmates and to make them assume responsibilities, too. The knowledge that prisoners have rights which are often abused has been instrumental as well in the creation in many states of an ombudsman.

An *ombudsman* in Scandinavian countries—the word is

Sing Sing: New York.

Swedish—is an appointed official who hears and investigates complaints against the government by private citizens. In Minnesota, the post of Ombudsman for Corrections was created shortly after the Attica revolt made national news. He could look into complaints made by prisoners against the prison system. He headed a staff of five. He could decide matters ranging from missing Christmas packages to unfair parole board decisions.

"A lot of staff people resent the idea of an ombudsman," one corrections official says. "But it's becoming popular because the evidence that prisoners' rights are violated is so indisputable."

Since when have prisoners had rights?

One concrete and far-reaching development in corrections has been prisoners' increasing use of the courts.

Why? Perhaps the wide publicity given Supreme Court decisions since 1950 that involve other areas of human rights was one reason. "Within a decade," Leonard Orland points out, "the Supreme Court prohibited racial segregation, guaranteed equal voting rights, and underscored the rights of criminal suspects being interrogated by the police. As a result prisoners developed an incredible legal sensitivity."

No doubt the availability of legal assistance programs helped, too. In any case, courts all the way up to the United States Supreme Court have increased prisoner rights in many areas. Prisoners now have legal avenues if prison life is brutal, more freedom to practice religion, increased rights to research their own cases, increased rights to hearings and to due process for parole violations.

Many programs within prison walls look to the day when the inmate will once again be a member of society. Thus, over half the states in this country, as well as the federal government, have adopted some variety of prerelease program.

In Colorado, for example, there is a five-week program for inmates about to be paroled. "The program is built," one writer explains, "on the premise that an inmate about to be released has many concrete and practical problems. Time and effort are spent attempting to alleviate some of these, i.e., clearing up drivers' licenses, obtaining Social Security Cards and issuing identification cards.

Many men who come through the Center have legal difficulties, and assistance is provided through local bar associations. Local professional people and businessmen give their time to discuss such problems as "how to obtain a job," "how to keep a job," "wardrobe tips," and "how to buy a car."

The centers have athletic teams. Visits from families are encouraged; mail is not censored. Men are assigned rooms and given their own keys. They wear civilian clothing. There are no bars on the windows. There are no guards.

Most prerelease centers, like the other reforms in the first group of proposals, involve changes within the prison. They bring members of the community inside prison walls.

The second class of prison reform proposals bring the prisoners into the community. They call for replacing the prison with some sort of alternative. Instead of changing the lives, routines, or powers of prison inmates, they try to bring inmates out from behind bars.

Reformers whose proposals fall into this category argue that only when surrounded by people who don't rob banks or forge checks can lawbreakers feel pressure to conform to the law. They also argue that within the community a variety of resources exist—medical and psychiatric clinics, social service agencies, volunteer pools—which have until now been underused in the attempt to reduce crime.

Among these reform proposals are:

—expanded parole and probation services
—halfway houses
—work-release programs
—programs of pretrial intervention

Many of those who advocate "community treatment" have been harshly critical of the American prison system. Yet, most of their suggestions do involve some sort of incarceration.

The Peoria Community Correctional Center, is one example of a community-based program. It is housed in a modern, light-colored building with big picture windows and a deeply slanted roof. There is a large recreation area with a pool table, television, refrigerator, and dining room. Staff offices are on the second floor.

The 45 residents sleep in one room, dormitory style. The beds can be partitioned off. Each man has a bed, dresser, and wardrobe. In fact, the residents can have anything else they want in their rooms, except alcohol, drugs, or sex. Men who have been there the longest enjoy more privileges.

Everyone at the Center has a job. Programs which allow prisoners to work and earn money are called *work release* and are a prime ingredient of most community-based treatment.

"Most of the men stay about six months," one counselor

A resident at the Peoria Center in Brimfield playing Eight Ball.

told us. "They work as welders or in auto body repair shops or warehouses. And some drive trucks in Illinois and a lot do construction."

The money each resident makes is deposited in his own account. He works with a counselor to draw up a budget. Some men need to support their families. Some have debts to pay off. Most of them take some spending money each week. In addition, they pay $35 a week for room and board.

Before coming to the Correctional Center, Arthur Baker had been at an honor farm in southern Illinois where restrictions were light. He felt he was treated more like an adult there than he was at the Center.

"But I was paid about $7.50 a month," he said. "Here I got $2,900 in the bank."

Most work-release jobs are menial. Stoop labor in California fields, dishwashing in restaurants, janitorial work; these unskilled, nonunion jobs paying the minimum wage are more representative than the $9.50 an hour steam-fitter or assistant television producer sometimes featured in work-release publicity.

Still, inmates often say that work release is the best thing about the community-based treatment programs.

Work release has selling points for other groups, too. For one thing, it is economical. The California Department of Corrections had 1,071 inmates on work-release jobs from 1966 to 1970. Of the $840,000 they earned, the state took almost half: $200,000 for "cost of care," $100,00 for "administration and supervision," and $100,000 for taxes.

Those on work release bought their own clothes. They received no "gate money" when they were released and that alone saved California over $72,000.

Employers benefit as well. Inmates must abide by prison rules, so it is unlikely that they will be late, have a hangover, miss a day, or join a union. They are a source of good, cheap labor for nonunion employers.

Until shortly before our visit to the Peoria Center, the halfway house had another program which the inmates considered vital. It was a program of furloughs.

In American prisons the *furlough* is a short leave granted to prisoners. While on furlough they can return home, take care of family business, or just relax.

"Take a guy coming out of prison after 15 or 20 years," one ex-con said. "He doesn't know how to dial a telephone call or order a meal for himself. A furlough gives him the chance to adjust slowly."

At the Peoria Center, Art Baker was scheduled to leave on a furlough of his own. But an election was coming up. Furlough programs were front page news. In California, the escape rate for prisoners on furlough had hit 15%. In Washington, D.C.,

FBI agents caught a convicted murderer at Union Station. Out on a 12-hour furlough, the agents found him with a sawed-off shotgun—and a one-way ticket to New York City. When one candidate discovered that the State of Illinois was allowing a well-known murderer—not Baker—to attend college classes unguarded and unescorted, he felt he had a ready-made campaign issue.

Finally, the Illinois Department of Corrections felt forced to suspend all furloughs—including Baker's.

"I was angry when they told me what happened," Baker said. "I didn't believe that the state stopped them. I was really hot about it. Those programs are beautiful. They actually keep a man's family together."

A month later the furlough program began again at the Center. But murderers were now excluded. The comment of one assistant to the Director of the Illinois Department of Corrections, showed how difficult it is to administer controversial programs.

"Murderers are our best risks," he said. "There are usually far fewer repeaters among them than the petty criminals. These people were carefully selected. We weren't just throwing murderers out into the streets without screening. But it made people angry. And the only way we're going to be able to keep these programs going is when the average guy thinks it's okay."

Public opinion is a problem for prison reformers. Very understandably, people have a gut fear of rapists, murderers, burglars, and even forgers. The idea of having them next door or down the street is disturbing.

Originally, the Peoria Center was to be located in Peoria. But when the families living nearby found out about it, they put pressure on city officials. They threatened court action. Finally, the center was forced to move to Brimfield, a small town outside the city limits.

"Sweet joint" and "community-based" treatment—both involve some type of confinement. But in the last 20 years, still another group of reformers has emerged. Joined by an increasing number of penologists, criminologists, sociologists, politicians, this group feels that *no* program which involves forced confinement can be effective. They believe that prison can neither control crime nor rehabilitate the small percentage of lawbreakers unfortunate enough to have been caught, convicted, and sent behind bars. Their slogan is "Break down the walls."

"No one has been able to run a decent prison," says Robert Sommer in his 1976 book, *The End of Imprisonment.* "Not the Quakers, not the Soviets, not the conservatives or liberals, not the federal government, not the state governments and not the counties. There is something basically wrong with the idea of forcibly removing lawbreakers from society, bringing them together in a single location and placing them under the domination of keepers for long periods."

In his ruling in a 1972 Wisconsin case dealing with prison mail censorship, Federal District Judge James Doyle wrote, "I am persuaded that the institution of prison probably must end. In many respects it is as intolerable within the United States as was the institution of slavery, equally brutalizing to all involved, equally toxic to the social system, equally subversive of the brotherhood of man, even more costly by some standards and probably less rational."

To this cluster of critics sometimes known as the "abolitionists"—those who want to abolish prisons—even the best halfway houses are not the answer. As the American Friends Service Committee points out, "Call them 'community treatment centers' or what you will, if human beings are involuntarily confined in them, they are prisons."

Moderate abolitionists argue that present-day prisons could serve as diagnostic departments. They would analyze each incoming inmate's needs and suggest a course of treatment. One offender might work in the prison and return home at night. Another might work outside and return to prison at night. Another might live and work outside the prison but return to the institution periodically.

Inmate photo.

Others have suggested traditional communities where willing convicts could serve their time with minimal restraints on their freedom. Some even suggest using abandoned ghost towns.

As it stands today, offenders commit crimes against the state rather than against people. The state avenges the wrong. A man who loses $5,000 in a robbery often never sees that money again. So, some have proposed that in place of punishment a convicted criminal be required to pay back his victim. Under this system fines would be based on the severity of the offense and the offender's ability to pay. Community supervisors would see to it that the inmates abided by the new requirement.

There are others who go further. "If the starting point is that prisons are intrinsically evil," writes radical abolitionist Jessica Mitford, "then the first principle of reform should be to have as few [convicts] as possible confined and for as short a time as possible." The last chapter of Mitford's book illustrates what is sometimes called the "radical abolitionist position." Certainly it is representative in much of its reasoning and many of its recommendations; for that reason, a brief summary should be useful.

Although "few would argue that prison rehabilitates, the proponent of abolition will, however, meet with deeply felt objections," writes Mitford. " 'My God, if you let all those killers, rapists, thugs, burglars on the streets, it wouldn't be safe to venture out!' "

To rebut that argument, Mitford reminds us that only the tiniest fraction of lawbreakers are in prison; that murderers are least likely to repeat their crimes; that 95% of sex offenders have been sentenced for nonviolent activities like indecent exposure.

"The notion," she writes, "that 75 percent, or 80 percent or 90 percent of the prison population could be freed tomorrow without danger to the community finds amazingly wide acceptance in prison administration circles."

While she recognizes the problem of deciding who the dangerous 10 or 20% would be, she recommends release of the rest as a giant step forward.

While she accepts the estimate that narcotics addicts are responsible for much street crime—about 50% of the property crime in New York City—she offers the American Civil Liberties Union solution for that problem: adopt the English system under which "heroin and other drugs are legally prescribed . . . thus eliminating the demand for black market heroin."

She dismisses the idea that prisons deter and asks the

question: what would happen if we were to abolish prisons entirely? And she points to Jerome Miller's program in Massachussetts, for some clues.

Dr. Miller, while commissioner of the Department of Youth Services in Massachusetts in 1969–71, cut the population of juvenile prisons in that state from 1,200–1,500 to about 80–100. The prisoners were released to their own homes or placed in foster homes. Some of the older boys and girls were encouraged to find their own apartments and were given some spending money. Only a few, considered "seriously assaultive" and "disturbed" were kept in custody.

Reports showed no increase in overall juvenile crime rates for Massachusetts but instead what Miller called "a dramatic drop in the amount of violence among those committed to the department." And further research as the decade progressed, at least demonstrated that the crime rate for juveniles was not affected.

Mitford also approves proposals aimed at reducing the power of authorities.

> all down the line, at reducing prison populations and at restoring to prisoners . . . constitutional rights.
> Sentences . . . should be vastly reduced in length. While there should be a great many educational, medical, psychiatric, vocational and other services available to prisoners . . . the prisoner would be free to take them or leave them, his decision in no way affecting length of time served. Parole . . . should be abolished and replaced by unsupervised release—again, with a vast range of "helping" services available on a voluntary basis to the men or women coming out of prison.

We don't quote Jessica Mitford, who after all is a generalist and journalist, because of her great expertise, although *Kind and Usual Punishment* is useful and interesting. We quote her because her views are representative of a large body of those interested in corrections reform.

The only opportunity these inmates have to watch television is when they are permitted to exercise in the yard.

Are there any programs at all other than the Massachusetts experiment which incorporate these views?

Well, not really. There are, however, programs which offer alternatives to confinement and where lawbreakers have a measure of freedom in building a course of treatment.

One alternative to imprisonment is probation—the convicted offender remains at liberty, but under the supervision of a probation officer, and in accordance with conditions set by the sentencing judge. In Rochester, Minnesota, for example, there is Probational Offenders Rehabilitation Training, or PORT. PORT takes convicted criminals through a five-stage classification system which involves a variety of institutions ranging from the Minnesota Department of Vocational Rehabilitation to the local community college.

• In Michigan, a similar program has been designed for repeat offenders. This is significant; model programs are too often reserved for model prisoners.

• Instead of sending lawbreakers to prison, a number of states have required criminals to pay back their victims. In Minnesota, a restitution program negotiates contracts between offenders and victims. When both parties agree, the lawbreaker goes to a Restitution Center to fulfill his part of the bargain. A program in Joliet, Illinois, sentences first time offenders to specific jobs.to enable them to repay victims.

• A number of programs experiment with the substitution of public service for the prison sentence. One, the Alternative Community Service Program in Multnomah County, Oregon, has assigned thousands of offenders to work with the blind, prepare food for the needy, do maintenance and construction work for public buildings.

Another example of this kind of experiment occurred in Phoenix, Arizona. There, a physician facing a sentence for selling amphetamines was sentenced to serve seven years as practicing physician in Tombstone, which then had no doctor at all. In Chicago, a 19 year old burglar with a reputation as a street fighter was assigned to a program at the county jail where he taught boxing.

Some programs in other countries show that there are workable alternatives to the prison sentence. All countries have prisons. But the United States sentences more people to prison than almost any other country—about 200 persons per 100,000 in the population, or ten times the rate of a country like Holland. American sentences are also the longest in the world. Recently, one corrections official went to an international conference on corrections in Geneva, Switzerland.

"They all had one recommendation to make to the Americans," he said to us when he returned. " 'Cut your sentences by two-thirds.' "

There are countries whose punishments are quite different from our own as this clipping from the May 6, 1979 *New York Times* makes clear.

Pakistanis Sentence 2 Robbers
To Amputation of Hand and Foot

LAHORE, Pakistan, May 6 (Reuters) — Two bank robbers have been sentenced to have their right hands and left feet amputated in the first such decision since the introduction of strict Islamic law, the Associated Press of·Pakistan said today..

Tayyab Ahmed and Sikandar Masih were convicted by an Islamic court of having robbed a bank in Shwal, 100 miles from Lahore, the agency said.

Laws allowing for the amputation of hand and foot for theft, stoning to death for adultery and whipping for Moslems who drink alcohol were put into effect by the military Government in February as part of a strict Islamic legal system.

Such sentences are alien to Americans. But we can learn from other countries.

In Egypt, some convicts may receive permission from the court to pay their penalties by working for the state. Since prisons are rather primitive in Egypt, this has been a popular alternative.

In Sweden, the furlough is an inmate's right, not a privilege. While Swedish authorities recognize the risks of a furlough program, they believe inmates should keep in close touch with family and relatives. After serving part of their sentences, Swedish inmates are eligible for as much as 72 hours off at a stretch. They can go to funerals, visit sick relatives, or go home for weddings or the harvest.

Swedish prisoners also have the right to look for jobs outside the prison if those within the prison shops don't satisfy them.

In England, most convicted criminals are not sent to prison—in fact, in 1975 only 34% served time. Fines accounted for 50% of the sentences in 1977. Probation is another alternative.

A recent innovation is a sentence of community service. Judges may order offenders to work for 40 to 240 unpaid hours in jobs such as assisting elderly and disabled persons, building and helping to run playgrounds, and working in hospitals.

About 12,000 work orders were made in 1977 and the number continues to grow. A judge might also decide to hand down a suspended sentence of not more than two years.

But for America to restructure its prison system, there would have to be a great deal of public pressure. There isn't. In fact, as we look through the books and articles written about prisons in the late 1970's, one thing is clear. The conclusion that nothing works—that prisons neither rehabilitate nor deter—has become more and more respectable. But the American system of criminal justice reflects American values. This must be true no matter how "progressive" are the values of judges and local officials in Michigan or Minnesota or Rhode Island. Thus, even the most radical reformers in American corrections dedicate themselves to achieving limited change. It is the kind of change the public will accept.

"Sure," says one convict quoted by Jessica Mitford, "prisons should be abolished. But don't let up on reform. If I've got cancer, don't wait for the definitive cure before treating me."

"Even if every reform proposal suggested in this book were adopted tomorrow," wrote Leonard Orland at the end of *his* proposals for change, "I do not believe that prisons would become pleasant places or that crime would be materially reduced. Why, then, bother? The answer, I submit, lies not in what we can do to reduce crime but in what we can do to civilize what we do to prisoners on the doubtful premise that prison can prevent crime."

And Charles Silberman, who spent six years studying the criminal justice system on a Ford Foundation grant, says, "Reform is essential for our sake, not just for the sake of the inmates and guards . . . the character of any society is judged by the way that society treats the least of its members."

Even those most pessimistic about the value of our prison system will settle for less than total revolution. "Such change," says one of them, "can come only when our views are shared by a good part of the population. I'm not holding my breath."

10

A Last Word

When we first began writing this book, Tina had just begun serving a three to five for armed robbery. As we write this last chapter, she is on parole. By the time you read about her, she will be living and working in a town in central Illinois.

She never thought much of prison life. "I think it's rotten. There are some here who should be locked up—but not like this. We got to be stuck in the rooms in that hot weather. We gotta be told when to eat, when to sleep, when to work, when to lay down. That really bugs you."

Tina's resentment of prison life may not win her much sympathy. For many she forfeited her right to our concern by aiming a gun at the head of a law-abiding citizen.

But some questions should concern us: Has Tina's stay at Dwight been useful to us? That is, will it keep her from committing crimes? Has it served as a lesson and thus a deterrent to others who might break the law?

Debating such issues can be exciting. But as we do so, let us try not to lose ourselves in the game of academic debate.

Just as we were correcting galleys for this book, two pris-

"...ELL THE GOVERNOR NOT TO SWEAT IT — WE'LL HAVE ALL MURDER, MUTILATION, BRUTALITY, RAPE AND MAYHEM BACK TO THE NORMAL ACCEPTABLE LEVELS IN NO TIME!"

When the bloodiest riot since Attica broke out in the New Mexico State Penitentiary, Patrick Oliphant drew this frequently reprinted cartoon.

oners overpowered a guard at the New Mexico State Penitentiary outside Santa Fe, and set in motion a 36 hour chain of violence and destruction which dramatized the urgent need to find alternatives. Taking control of the administration building, cutting phone lines to isolate watchmen, a group of inmates set fires throughout the prison, then went on a rampage of —according to *Newsweek*—"beheading, hanging, torching and rape."

Thirty-three inmates were killed. Unlike the rebellion at Attica, the violence this time was initiated by convicts.

The plain fact is that the great majority of inmates at Santa Fe were as horrified as anyone at the violence, they paid a price far beyond what judges and juries had decided was appropriate for their crimes, and, as the Oliphant cartoon points out, such violence is an inescapable part of prison life. And Santa Fe, like Attica nine years earlier, reminds us that for hundreds of thousands of men and women, the race to find alternatives to prison life is no game.

But what alternatives do we have?

We have written *Doing Time* to help answer this question, both for the readers and for ourselves. Our conclusion has been depressing. We do not feel prisons protect us at all.

Prisons keep such a small percentage of lawbreakers away from the rest of us that were every prison to be abolished tomorrow we would hardly notice the effect on the crime rate. There is a distinct possibility that such a move would, in the long run, decrease crime.

Prisons are schools of crime; at the same time, they are arenas of violence which condition inmates to respond violently to any insult whether imagined or real. They penalize the poor and the minorities. Victims of class and racial discrimination at every step of our criminal justice system, minorities are disproportionately represented in prison.

It would be unfair to say that most prison officials have stopped believing in rehabilitation. Actually, one 1974 survey of prison administrators indicated that 63% felt rehabilitation could work.

It is hardly a reassuring figure. How confident would we be of airplanes if only 63% of our pilots thought planes *could* fly?

We do not believe that prisons either rehabilitate or deter. Does that mean that nowhere in this country are there inmates who have responded to the job-training or counseling programs which have occupied corrections officials for a generation? Does it mean that there is no one who decided not to commit a crime because he was afraid of being caught?

No. There are probably thousands of inmates who have been rehabilitated and just as many who have been deterred. But, do the good effects outweigh the bad? Those who try to make that case do not persuade us.

What do we suggest?

First, we believe that prisons are vastly overcrowded. With all the talk of community-based corrections, by 1980 the prison population had taken an alarming surge upward, reaching a record high of 300,000. In some states, the number of inmates has increased by 45% in only three years, with a corresponding increase in violence and brutality. By decriminalizing many of the so-called crimes without victims, particularly drug and sex offenses (excluding rape, a crime of violence), we would take a major first step in reducing the number of those incarcerated.

It should be apparent that we are highly suspicious of both the effectiveness and competence of the American system of parole and probation. We are also aware of the dangers of allowing a politically appointed board decide which of the men and women still in American prisons are dangerous.

But here we part company with some of the radical abolitionists who believe in unsupervised release. We think a mechanism should be set up to release almost all inmates except those who have demonstrated a history of repeated or extreme violence—but we would place them under some sort of probationary system. This is not as revolutionary an idea as it might seem. A century ago, all convicted lawbreakers were sent to prison. Now only about one-third serve time. We want to accelerate that trend.

Experiments in New Zealand and in the United States have shown that contracts of restitution between criminal and victim can be substituted for the prison sentence. Such contracts, in addition to a system of fines and work for the state, should fulfill our desire to punish lawbreakers in a way which satisfies those most directly hurt by the lawbreaker.

At the same time, a variety of resources—therapy, counseling, job training, and placement—of the types described in Chapter Nine should be available. We believe the convicted lawbreaker should have as wide a variety of options as possible in deciding which to use. But we believe he should have to choose something.

Robert Martinson, whose landmark study we have already mentioned, believes that with the prison population reduced by four-fifths we would have enough "money to provide almost one-to-one supervision of offenders in the community." He favors substituting parole and probation for almost all prison sentences. We agree.

Does this mean we oppose programs like the Peoria Community Correctional Center? By no means. The inmate who cautioned Jessica Mitford about not letting up on reform had a point. In no state would the kind of program we advocate win legislative approval. Thus, to the extent that halfway houses, minimum security prisons, self-government within prison, ombudsmen, work release, and furloughs reduce the brutality and hopelessness of the fortress prison, we are for them.

We would like legislators to work for a sharp reduction in the length of sentences. But at the same time, we would like legislators to focus on other areas of American life in the effort to reduce crime. One reason for the bitterness of much of the debate about our prisons is that we expect far too much of them.

Whatever program we develop for the few lawbreakers we manage to convict will have little effect on the crime rate. To ban handguns, to model drug legislation on the English system, to tackle the problem of redistributing income—these are steps which we think would dramatically decrease crime.

Exploring these ideas, though, is beyond the scope of this book. *Doing Time* has been concerned with exploring one American institution: the prison. How did society arrive at the idea? What purpose is it designed to serve? What is the evidence that it actually serves that purpose? What alternatives do those opposing it offer as replacements?

Webster's New World Dictionary defines *institution* as "an organization having a social, educational or religious purpose, as a school, church, hospital, reformatory, etc."

Some people believe it is unpatriotic to question institutions. We believe it is healthy. Schools, churches—and prisons—were thought up by men and women. Like everyone else, these men and women made mistakes.

Unlike the mistakes that we make, however, the mistakes of social reformers can be extremely damaging to the lives of millions of people. The lesson of prison history is that the most brilliant and compassionate thinkers—Jeremy Bentham, for example, or Beccaria—can generate ideas in the quiet of their studies which, hundreds of years later, result in the chattering machine guns of a prison revolt. No one has yet come up with a solution to the crime problem. If we hope to make progress in the future, we must be willing to experiment with new suggestions. But we would also be wise to take all ideas for corrections reform with one and probably two grains of salt. Even our ideas.

Overleaf: Inmate photo, Green Haven State Prison; New York.

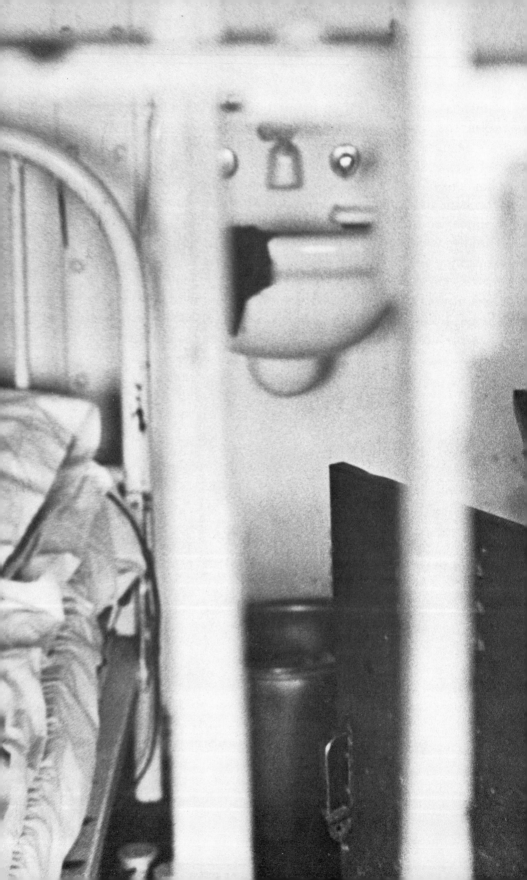

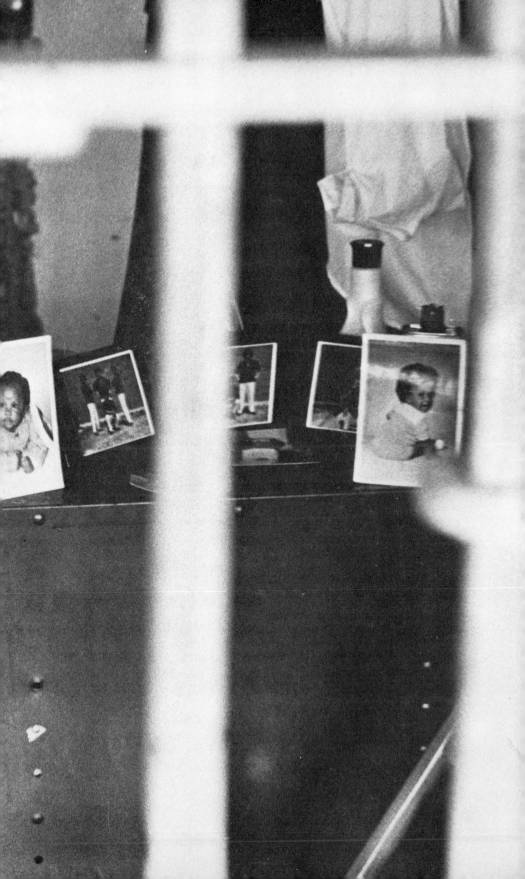

Bibliography

GENERAL

American Friends Service Committee. *Struggle for Justice.* New York: Hill & Wang, 1971.

Bagdikian, Ben and Dash, Leon. *The Shame of the Prisons.* New York: Pocket Books, 1972.

Clark, Ramsey. *Crime in America: Observations on Its Nature, Causes, Prevention and Control.* New York: Simon & Schuster, 1970.

Fogel, David. ". . . We Are the Living Proof . . .". Cincinnati: W. H. Anderson Company, 1975.

Goldfarb, Ronald and Singer, Linda R. *After Conviction.* New York: Simon & Schuster, 1973.

Harris, Janet. *Crisis in Corrections: The Prison Problem.* New York: McGraw-Hill, 1973.

Horowitz, Elinor. *Capitol Punishment, U.S.A.* Philadelphia: Lippincott, 1973.

Liston, Robert H. *The Edge of Madness: Prisons and Prison Reform in America.* New York: Franklin Watts, 1972.

Mitford, Jessica. *Kind and Usual Treatment.* New York: Alfred Knopf, 1973.

Orland, Leonard. *Prisons: Houses of Darkness.* New York: The Free Press, 1975.

Silberman, Charles E. *Criminal Violence, Criminal Justice.* New York: Random House, 1978.

Sloan, Irving J. *Youth and the Law.* Dobbs Ferry, New York: Ocean Publications, 1970.

TEXTBOOKS, REPORTS AND SCHOLARLY WORKS

Carney, Louis. *Introduction to Correctional Science.* New York: McGraw-Hill, 1974.

Carter, Robert M. and Wilkins, Leslie, eds. *Probation, Parole and Community Corrections,* 2nd edition. New York: John Wiley & Sons, 1976.

Clemmer, Donald. *The Prison Community.* New York: Holt, Rinehart and Winston, 1968.

Conrad, John P. *Crime and Its Correction: An International Survey of Attitudes and Practices.* Berkeley: University of California Press, 1970.

Dressler, David, ed. *Readings in Criminology and Penology,* 2nd edition. New York: Columbia University Press, 1972.

Official Report of the New York State Commission On Attica. New York: Bantam Books, 1972.

The President's Commission on Law Enforcement and the Administration of Justice. *The Challenge of Crime in a Free Society.* Washington, D.C.: U.S. Government Printing Office, 1967.

———. *Task Force Report: Crime and Its Impact—An Assessment.* Washington, D.C.: U.S. Government Printing Office, 1967.

Sutherland, Edwin H. and Cressey, Donald R. *Criminology,* 9th edition. Philadelphia: Lippincott, 1974.

PERSONAL ACCOUNTS OR NARRATIVE

Bennett, James V. *I Chose Prison.* New York: Alfred Knopf, 1970.

Duffy, Clinton D. with Jennings, Dean. *San Quentin Story.* New York: Doubleday, 1950.

Hunt, Morton. *The Mugging.* New York: Atheneum, 1972.

Pell, Eve, et al., eds. *Maximum Security: Letters from California's Prisons.* New York: Dutton, 1972.

Smith, Edgar. *Getting Out.* New York: Coward, McCann & Geoghegan, 1972.

HISTORY

Babington, Anthony. *The English Bastille: A History of Newgate Gaol and Prison Conditions in Britain, 1188–1902.* New York: St. Martin's Press, 1971.

Barnes, Harry E. *The Story of Punishment,* 2nd edition revised. Montclair, New Jersey: Patterson Smith, 1972.

Beccaria, Cesare. *An Essay on Crime and Punishment.*

De Beaumont, G. and De Tocqueville, A. *On the Penitentiary System in the United States.*

Earle, Alice M. *Curious Punishments of ByGone Days* (1896). Publication 33: Patterson Smith Reprint Series in Criminology, Law Enforcement and Social Problems. Montclair, New Jersey: Patterson Smith, 1969.

Eriksson, Torsten. *The Reformers: An Historical Survey of Pioneer Experiments in the Treatment of Criminals.* Amsterdam: Elsevier Publishers, 1976.

Howard, John. *The State of Prisons* (1780).

Rothman, David J. *The Discovery of the Asylum: Social Order and Disorder in the New Republic.* Boston: Little, Brown, 1971.

Index

Academy of the Fists, 35
Adams, John, 37
Agnew, Spiro, 80
alcoholism, 11-12; arrests due to, 74
American Civil Liberties Union, 134
appeals process, 112
Arizona, 137
arraignment, 81
arrest, 9, 67-70, 71, 73, 74, 75-76, 84, 85, 112; prejudice in, 76
Attica, N.Y. prison riot, 63-65, 91, 126, 141
attorneys, 14, 70, 77, 81; court appointed, 77; plea bargaining, 78-80
Auburn (New York), 50-52 (see also silent system)
Australia, 42; Norfolk Island penal colony, 42, 58
Ayinlungu, 19

bail, 70, 71, 77, 112
Baker, Arthur, 123, 129-131
Beccaria, Cesare Bonesana, the Marchese di, 34-38, 56, 66, 144
Benefit of Clergy, 26-27
Bentham, Jeremy, 43-45, 145
Berman, Dr. Allen, 92

Bishop's Court, 26
black offenders, 76, 77, 82, 91-92; abuse of, 92; parole, 82; sentences, 82
blood feud, 22-23
Bloom, Stanton, 81
Boston, 50, 75
Botany Bay, 42
Bridewell, 29
Brockway, Zebulon, 60
Burger, Chief Justice Warren, on outmoded prisons, 16

California, 55, 61, 74, 76, 81, 84, 101, 130; San Quentin, 100; Soledad prison, 92
capital punishment, 19, 22, 23, 24, 30-32, 34, 37, 44-45, 46, 70, 81, 82, 109
Carlson, Norman, 120
Catherine the Great, 37
censorship of mail, 63, 65, 127, 132
chain gang, 59
Chaneles, Sol, 100
Cherry Hill, Pennsylvania prison, 48-51, 55
Chessman, Caryl, 102
Chicago, Illinois, 75, 78, 137
Church courts, Middle Ages, 26-28, 30
Cincinnati, National Prison Congress of 1870, 59, 87

Citizens Inquiry on Parole and Criminal Justice, 1974, 113
clan, 22
Clark, Ramsey, 12, 113, 118
coed prisons, 124-125
Coke, Lord Chief Justice Edward, 32
Colorado, prerelease program, 127
community based treatment, 123, 128-132, 133-134, 137, 138-139, 143-144
confinement (see prison)
congregate system, 50-52
conjugal visits, 107
Connecticut, 54, 77; congregate prison, 52
convict caste system, 104
Cook, Fred J., 74
Cook, Captain James, 42
Cook County Public Defender's Office, Chicago, 81
corporate crime, 68, 71, 73 (see also white collar crime)
correctional officers, 92-94, 102, 104, 111, 126; and prisoner homosexuality, 107; at Dwight, 98-99, 105
country club prisons, 98
courts, 80-81, 126-127; congestion, 78-79; inequities, 76-77
Cressey, Donald, 68
crime, 10, 14-15, 16-17, 19-20, 22-32, 34, 36, 37, 40, 45, 47-48, 50, 55, 56, 57, 68, 80-85, 128, 133; arson, 76; assault, 70, 76; bank robbery, 73, 104, 110; breaking and entering, 76; bribery, 71, 73, 75, 80; burglary, 70-71, 73, 84; capital, 19, 22, 23, 24, 30-32, 34, 37, 44, 46, 70, 81, 82, 109; causes of, 12, 13, 14-15, 57, 67-69, 84, 145; decriminalization of, 142-143; deterrence, 13-14; felony, 70, 79, 80; forgery, 104; misdemeanor, 70, 71, 82; murder, 70, 104, 107-108, 124, 130-131, 134; police, as lawbreakers, 75-76, 84; prevention of, 13, 14, 84, 128, 144, 145; recidivism, 61, 66, 108, 113, 118, 124, 140; school for, 16, 142; stealing, 75, 82; victimless, 74, 143; white collar, 71, 73 (see also crime bribery)
criminals, study of, 56, 57, 62
Criminal Justice Act of 1779, 41, 59
Criminal Man, The (Lombroso), 56
criminologist, 71, 132
Crofton, Walter, 58, 60, 66
crucifixion, 23 (see also punishments)

Darwin, Charles, effect on Lombroso, 56
death penalty (see capital punishment)
Death Row, 109
debtors, 32, 33-34, 47, 53
dehumanization, prisons, 15-16, 18
deterrence, 13, 22, 37, 41, 118, 140; criticism of theory of, 14, 15, 16, 134-135, 139, 142
diagnostic clinics, 62
Diderot, Denis, 38
Dickens, Charles, on Cherry Hill, 48
discharge (see release)
Discovery of the Asylum, The (Rothman), 18
discrimination, 16-17, 37, 71, 77, 81-82, 121; against ex-convict, 114, 115; arrests, 82; bail, 77; dismissals, 77; indictments, 77; parole, 82; sentencing, 82
Doyle, Judge James (see prison, abolitionists)
Draco, 23
drugs and crime, 73, 104, 107, 124-125, 134-135, 143; English system, 134-135; Knapp Commission, 76
drunkenness, 12, 74
Dutch system, 39-40
Dwight Correctional Center, Illinois, 9-10, 13-14, 85, 91-92, 96-99, 105, 108; education, 87, 90, 101; inmate relationships, 102, 105, 107; routine, 88-90

Eastern Penitentiary (Pennsylvania) (see Cherry Hill)
Edward VI, 29
Egypt, 20th century alternative to prison, 138
Elam, 19, 22
Elizabeth I, 30-31
Elmira, 60-61
End of Imprisonment, The (Sommer), 132
England, 25, 29-30, 32, 45, 138; Criminal Justice Act of 1779, 41-42; House of Correction, 29-30; John Howard, 38-40, 42; hulks, 41; Navy, use of galley slaves, 30; Panopticon, 43-44; Poor Law, 29; public service as alternative, 138; wergeld, 24

Essay on Crime and Punishment, An (Beccaria), 36

ex-convicts, 108; credit problems, 116; discrimination against, 114-116; furloughs, 130; prerelease programs, 127; readjustment to outside, 114

executions (see capital punishment)

exile, 32, 34

Farrell, Barry, on Walla Walla experiment, 125

Father of the Penitentiary System, 45

Federal Bureau of Investigation (F.B.I.), 70; crime rates, 119

Federal Bureau of Prisons, 82

Federal District Courts, 81

Federal Enforcement Agencies, 70

federal prisons, 70, 82, 132; libraries in, 102; statistics, 12

Felon, The (Irwin), 114

Finley, Reverend James B., 52-53

flogging (see punishment)

Florida, probation, 14-15, 77

Fogel, David, 93

fortress prison, 53, 61, 124, 144

Framingham Correctional Institution (Virginia), 124-125

"free time", Dwight, 89-90

furlough, 130, 144; abuse of, 91, 130-131; Sweden, 138

galley slaves, 30, 34

gambling, Knapp Commission, 76; Mafia, 73

gaol, 25, 38; conditions in, 25-26, 34, 109; criticism of, 34; Howard, 40; Oglethorpe, 32; disease in, 25-26, 32, 53, 109

George II, 33

Georgia, Oglethorpe's colony, 33-34

Germanic tribes, 24

Gilmore, Gary, 70

good behavior, 82, 83, 104; Walter Crofton, 58; Alexander Maconochie, 58; National Prison Association, 59

guards, 52, 63, 94, 96, 101, 102, 104, 105-107, 111, 112, 125, 127; Dwight, 85, 89-90, 98-99; recruitment, 65, 91; salaries, 90, 93; torture by, 55; "trus-tees", 54; violence potential, 92-93 (see also correctional officers)

halfway houses, 123-124, 128-131, 144 (see also prison, alternatives)

hanging, 14, 26, 30-32, 37 (see also capital punishment)

Hawkins, Gordon, 113

health (see medical care)

Henry II, 25

Henry VIII, 28-30, 109

"hole", 94, 96, 98 (see also solitary confinement)

Holland, 39-40, 137

Holmesburg, 105-107

homosexuality, 42, 104-107

House of Correction (Bridewell), 29-30

Howard, John, 38-43, 66

hulks, 41, 42, 109

Illinois, 75, 78, 81, 120-121, 137; Illinois Law Enforcement Commission, 93; Peoria Community Correctional Center, 123-124, 128-131

immigrants, 19th century America, 54

indentured servants, 33-34, 42

indeterminate sentence, 82-84; Elmira (New York), 60; Alexander Maconochie, 58-59

Indiana State Prison, sentence study, 84

individualized treatment, 57, 87

injustice (see also discrimination), 84; arrest, 76, 82, 142; bail, 77; jury trial, 81; plea bargaining, 80; sentencing, 81; white collar crime, 71, 73

inmates, abuse of, 25-26, 30, 32, 34, 37, 38-39, 60, 62, 63, 102, 104, 121, 126-127, 140-141, 144; American prisons, 54-55, 92-93; Botany Bay (Australia), 42-43; hulks, 41-42, 109; medical experiments, 96-97; rights, *furlough* (see furlough); *ombudsman* (see ombudsman); *self-government*, 144; *violations of*, 126; *Walla Walla experiment*, 125; solitary confinement, 94-95 (see also solitary confinement); violence potential, 92; wages, 99-100

insanity, 57

Ireland, 58, 60

Irwin, John (*The Felon*), 114
isolation, 94, 96 (see also solitary confinement)
Italy, 34-37, 56

jail, 10-11, 70, 80
Jefferson, Thomas, 37
Journal of Criminal Law, 98
judges, 10, 70-71, 77, 81, 82, 83, 84, 85
jury trial, 70, 81
Justitia, 41
juveniles, 60, 69-70; discrimination, 76; Elmira (New York), 60-61; Massachusetts program, 135; Piedmont (California), 76; recidivism rates, 118, 120

Keenan, Assistant District Attorney Frank, 78
Kefauver, Senator Estes, Special Committee to Investigate Organized Crime in Interstate Commerce, 73
Kind and Usual Punishment (Mitford), 135
Kinsey, Alfred, 104-105
Knapp Commission 1971, 75-76
Koch, Mayor Edward (New York City), 84

law enforcement officers, 68-71, 73-77
lawyers (see attorneys)
legal assistance programs, 127
legal resources, 124
Life magazine, 125
Lombroso, Cesare, 56-57
Lorton (Virginia), Reformatory for the District of Columbia, 61
Louisiana, 92
Luger, Milton, 120
Lyle, Clement, 68

Maconochie, Captain Alexander, 58, 66; effects on American penal system, 111
Mafia, 73-74
Mafia! (Cook), 74
Manhattan, overload of cases, 78-79

"man-money", 24
marijuana, 70, 74
Martinson, Robert, 118, 143
Massachusetts, 120-121, 135; Framingham, 124-125
maximum security, 61, 88, 92
McNaughton rule, 57-58
medical care, 40, 96, 124, 135; in American prisons, 53, 62, 63, 96; experimentation on inmates, 96-97; in gaols, 25-26
medical experiments on inmates, 96-97
meditation, Quakers, 47
men's reformatory, 105-107
mentally retarded, 104
Michigan, 136-137
Miller, Dr. Jerome, 120-121; Massachusetts juvenile program, 134-135
minimum security, 61, 88, 144; reform, Framingham (Massachusetts), 124-125
Minnesota, 126, 137; PORT, 136
Mitford, Jessica, 18, 68, 76, 84, 134-135, 139, 144
Montesquieu, 36, 38
Morris, Norval, 18, 113
mutilation, 20, 23, 26, 27 (see also punishment, ancient)
Mynshal, Geoffrey, 34

National Council on Crime and Delinquency, 120
National Guard, 63
National Prison Association, Declaration of Principles, 1870, 59, 60
National Prison Congress of 1870, 59, 87
negotiated plea (see plea bargaining)
New Times, white collar crime vs. robberies, 73
New York, 60, 62, 65, 78-79, 80, 82, 84, 101, 110, 116, 118, 120, 134; Attica, 63, 65, 91, 126, 141; Auburn, 50-52; Elmira, 60-61; Knapp Commission, 76; prison without walls, 61; Rand Institute Study on bail, 77
New York magazine, on court overload, 78
New York Times, 125, 138
New Zealand, 143
Nixon's Task Force on Prisoner Rehabilitation, 102
Norfolk Island, 58
Norman kings, 24-25

Oglethorpe, James, 32-34
Ohio, 52-53, 59, 87
ombudsman, 125-126, 144
Open Prison, The (Chaneles), 100
organized crime, 73-74 (see also Mafia)
Orland, Leonard, 126-127, 139

Panopticon, 43-44
parole, 60, 96, 104, 110-112, 128, 135, 143-144; discrimination in, 82-84; National Prison Association, 59; prerelease programs, 127; rules of, 112; violations, 112-113, 127
parole boards, 60, 110-112, 124, 143
parole officers, 111-113
Patriotic Society of Berne, 37
patronage, 91
penal colonies, Botany Bay, 42; Georgia, 32-33; Norfolk Island, 58
penance, 27-28
penitentiary houses, 41
Pennsylvania, 46-50, 94; Cherry Hill, 48-49; Holmesburg, 105-107
penologists, 66, 132
Peoria Community Correctional Center (Illinois), 123-124, 128-131, 144
Persia, 23
pharmaceutical companies, 96-97
Philadelphia, Cherry Hill, 48-49; Father of the Penitentiary System, 45
Philadelphia Society for Alleviating the Miseries of Public Prisons, 46, 50, 66
Piedmont, California, 76
Pilsbury, Warden Amos, 54
Pittsburgh, Western Penitentiary, 48
plea bargaining, 10, 79, 80-81; Spiro Agnew, 80
police, 68-71, 73-77, 84
PORT (Probational Offenders Rehabilitation Training), 136
prerelease programs, 124, 127-131, 132-134, 139, 142; community opposition, 131; Egypt, 138; England, 138; Leonard Orland, 139; probation, 136; public service, 137; restitution, 133-134, 137; Sweden, 138
President's Crime Commission, on police honesty, 75
price fixing, 71 (see also white collar crime)

Principles of Criminology (Sutherland and Cressey), 68
prison, 10-12, 14-15, 16, 18, 30, 36-37, 52, 53-54, 60, 63, 65, 66, 69, 70, 76, 97, 120, 121; abolitionists, *Judge James Doyle,* 132-134; *Dr. Jerome Miller,* 120-121, 134; *Jessica Mitford,* 18, 68, 76, 84, 134-135; *Robert Sommer,* 132; administrators, 54, 71, 107, 142; admittance procedure, 9, 62; alternatives, 138-139; *community based treatment,* 123, 127-132, 133-134, 137, 138-139, 142-144; *fines,* 138-139; *ghost towns,* 133; *halfway houses,* 123-124, 128-131, 144; *work release,* 123-124, 128-131, 144; American prisons, 10; *Attica,* 63, 65; *Auburn,* 50; *Cherry Hill,* 48-50; *Dwight,* 87-92; *Elmira,* 60; *federal,* 12; *Framingham,* 124-125; *Massachusetts Women's Reformatory,* 61; *Michigan State Penitentiary,* 62; *South Carolina,* 15, 16; *state,* 12; *Walnut Street Jail,* 45, 46; *Western Penitentiary,* 48; architecture, 61, 107; Austria, 37; Botany Bay, 42-43; brutality in, 63, 102, 127; caste system, 104; cells, 14, 25, 38, 41-42, 43-44, 47, 48, 50, 52, 53-54, 92, 107, 108; classification of inmates, 61-62, 70-71, 81; clothing, 9, 65, 85, 107, 127, 130; co-ed, 124-125; congregate prisons, 50; conjugal visits, 107; critics of, *Milton Luger,* 120; *Jessica Mitford,* 18, 68, 76, 84, 134-135; *Norval Morris,* 18; *Quakers,* 132; *David Rothman,* 18; *Robert Sommer,* 132; economics of, 51, 52, 65, 97, 100, 102, 108; education in, 98-100; England, 32, 41-42, 45; *Jeremy Bentham,* 43-44; *Bridewell, House of Corrections,* 29-30; *gaols,* 25-26, 34, 38, 41; *John Howard,* 38-40, 42; *hulks,* 41; *Panopticon,* 43-44; escapes, 93, 110; Germanic tribes, 24; Holland, 39-40; homosexuality, 104-107; industry, 44, 47, 48, 52, 58, 59, 62-63, 93, 96-97, 98-100, 101, 116, 121, 135; *Attica,* 64; *Auburn,* 50-51; *Australian prison camps,* 43; *Cherry Hill,* 48, 51; *Dwight,* 87, 89, 98; *England,* 38-39; *Germany,* 30; *Holland,* 38; *job training,* 62, 98; Norfolk Island, 58; *pay,* 129; *racism,* 91; *Sweden,* 138; *Walnut Street Jail,* 47;

prison (*Continued*)
  inmates (see inmates); job training,
  100-101; juveniles, 76; libraries, 102,
  location of, 90-91; medical care in, 96;
  medical testing in, 96-97; National
  Prison Association, 59-60; New York
  Prison Commission, 55; Norfolk Island,
  58; population, 135, 143; problems of,
  14-15, 16-17, 98, 99-101, 107-108, 124,
  131, 137, 139, 141, 142, 145; punishment in, 94-95, 98; *Quakers,* 46; racial
  tension in, 63, 65; recidivism, 120; rehabilitation, 51 (see rehabilitation);
  Roman, 24; separate system, 48, 50-51;
  sex in, 104-107; *among inmates,* 34,
  105-107; smuggling in, 65, 73, 104, 107;
  solitary confinement, 94, 96; Spinnhaus, 30; trustee system, 54; violations
  of prisoners' rights in, 125-126; violence
  in, 16, 63, 102, 104, 105-107, 141-142;
  without walls, 61
prison inmates, caste system, 104
probation, 77, 80, 138, 143; alternative to
  prison, 128, 136-137
prosecutors, 79-81, 85
prostitution, 73, 74; in prison, 105,
  124-125
psychiatrists, 97, 98, 135
psychologists, 62, 87, 92, 96; role in rehabilitation, 97-98
psychosis, related to solitary confinement,
  96
public defender, 77, 81
public trials, Beccaria, 37
public opinion, effect on reforms, 131, 139
public service (see community based
  treatment)
punishment, 10, 13, 14, 16, 23, 31, 36-37,
  42-43, 44, 48, 50, 65, 91, 92; alternatives
  to prison (see prison, alternatives); ancient, 19, 22-23, 24; *mutilation,* 23;
  wer-geld, 24; *whipping,* 23; as deterrent,
  13-14; executions (see capital punishment); flogging, 28, 42, 47, 50, 52;
  Holland, 39-40; imprisonment (see
  prison); in Church courts, 27; in England, 26, 29, 38-39, 41-42, 45;
  transportation, 32-34; Quakers, 46-47;
  restitution (see restitution); retribution,
  14; sentence (see sentencing); silent

system, 52, 54-55; whipping, 23, 26, 28,
  29, 43, 46-47, 52, 55, 59, 93

Quakers, 46-47, 132

racial bias, 16, 17, 66, 76, 77, 82, 91, 142
racketeering, 73
Rand Institute Study, effect of bail on
  sentencing, 77
rape, 70, 76, 82; in prison, 104, 105-107
Rashliegh, Ralph, 42-43
recidivism, 61, 66, 108, 113, 118, 124, 140;
  effect of length of sentence, 120
recreation, Dwight, 90
reform, 24-25, 26, 29, 41, 57, 62, 66, 83, 96,
  107, 108, 131, 139, 143-145; American
  prisons, 48, 50, 55, 60, 87; Beccaria,
  13-14, 34-38; Jeremy Bentham, 43-
  45; Church, 26-28; community based
  treatment, 127-131, 138-139; Walter
  Crofton, 58; education, 62, 97-98; John
  Howard, 34, 38-40; job training, 62,
  99-101; Alexander Maconochie, 58;
  medical care, 62, 65, 96; National Prison
  Association (Ohio), 59; ombudsman,
  125-126, 143; Orland, Leonard, 139;
  parole (see parole); prerelease programs,
  124, 127; sentences, 66 (see also sentencing); Charles Silberman, 139;
  Spinnhaus, 30; *The State of Prisons*
  (Howard), 40; Walnut Street Jail, 48
rehabilitation, 14, 15, 28-29, 55, 65, 83, 90,
  96, 98, 108, 116, 118, 139, 140, 142,
  143; Criminal Justice Act of 1779, 41;
  critics of, 15; educational programs, 62,
  93, 98-99, 100-101, 102, 135; *Attica,* 65;
  Dwight, 87, 90, 101; *Elmira,* 61; *Walnut
  Street jail,* 47; halfway houses, 123-124;
  House of Corrections (Bridewell), 29;
  industry, 100; jobs, 99, 101; parole,
  111-113; prisoners in community,
  128-131; Spinnhaus, 29-30; "sweet
  joint," 124, 131; work release, 123-124
release, 109, 114, 135, 142; Walter Crofton, 58; Holland, 40; Alexander
  Maconochie, 58
religion, 20, 22, 23, 26-28, 41, 46, 47, 48,
  62, 94, 102, 127

Rentzel, Peter, 29-30
repeaters (see recividism)
restitution, 133-134, 137, 143
retribution, 10, 13, 14, 36; blood feud, 22-23; primitive tribal society, 22; wergeld, 24
Richardson, Elliot, 80
Ridley, Bishop, 29
Robinson, James, 120
Rome, 23
Rothman, David, 18
run-away child, 74, 84
rural prisons, 87, 90-92
Russia, 37, 42

salaries, guards, 90, 93
San Quentin, 100; brutality, 124
Scandinavian countries, 125-126
Schnur, Edwin, 74, 98
segregation, 94, 96
sentencing, 18, 45, 53, 66, 68-69, 70, 71, 77, 80, 81-82, 104, 119, 120, 124, 133-134, 135, 144; Spiro Agnew, 80; Beccaria, 37; differences in, 81-82; flat, 60, 82-85; Holland, 39; indeterminate, 82-85; juveniles, 69; length of, 137; plea bargaining, 79; reduced sentences, 109; release, 110-111; sanity/insanity, 57-58
separate system, 48, 50-51
sex, separation by, 47, 50, 53, 61
Shay's Rebellion, 68
Silberman, Charles, 16, 69, 85, 139
silent system (Auburn), 50-52, 59, 107; torture in, 54-55
slave trading, 68
Smith, Edgar, 102
Smith, Gerald, 120
smuggling, 104, 107; Attica, 65; Mafia, 73
socializing in prison, 62, 102, 104; homosexuality, 104-107
Society for the Promotion of Christian Knowledge, 34
sociologists, 66, 93-94, 97, 102, 132
Soledad prison (California), 92
solitary confinement, 41-42, 94-95; American prisons, 47-48, 50, 94, 96; Ireland, 58; Panopticon, 43-44
Sommer, Robert, 132

South Carolina, 16; Central Correctional Institution, 15
Sparta, 23
Spinnhaus, 30
Spirit of the Laws (Montesquieu), 36
spouses, 129, 131; conjugal visits, 107; divorces during terms, 114
staff, prison, 91-92, 95
starvation, 40; Australian prison camps, 43; gaols, 38
state government, 114-116, 132; parole boards, 110-111
State of Prisons, The (Howard), 40
state prisons, 12, 70
stealing, 82; President's Crime Commission, police honesty, 75
stocks, in America, 47
Sumerian law codes, 23
Sutherland, Edwin, 68, 71
Sutton, Willie, 110
Sweden, 138
"sweet joint", 124, 131
Switzerland, International Conference on Corrections (Geneva), 137

Theresa, Empress Maria, 37
Thompson, Governor James R. (Illinois), *on Agnew*, 80
ticket of leave, 59
Tina, 9-10, 13-14, 18, 67, 69-71, 85, 87-90, 97-99, 101, 102; parole, 140; rehabilitation, 108
torture, 29, 36-37; ancient civilization, 23; Cherry Hill (Pennsylvania), 48; silent system, 52, 54-55
transportation, 32-34, 37, 40-42, 58
treason, 70 (see also crime, capital)
trial, 70-71, 78-81, 84, 128; delays due to court congestion, 78-79; plea bargaining (see plea bargaining)
tribes, 22-23
"trustees", 54

Ulpian, 24
United States Bureau of Prisons, negative effects of jail, 120
United States Chamber of Commerce, 71
United States District Courts, 81

University of Rhode Island, 92
urban crime and criminals, 90-92
Utah, Gary Gilmore, 70; University of, 120

vagabonds, 28-29
victimless crime, 74, 143
violence potential, study, inmates and correctional officers, 92
violence, in prison, 16, 102, 104, 140-141; *Attica* (New York), 63, 141; *New Mexico State Penitentiary,* 140-141; in homosexuality, 105-107
violent criminal, 135; juveniles, 69; recidivism, 120
Virginia, 61, 81-82
visitation, Attica, 63, 65; congregate system, 52; conjugal visits, 107; Panopticon, 44; prerelease center, 127; rural prisons, 90-91; visitation rights, 124; Walnut Street Jail, 47
vocational training, 100-101

wages, prisoner, 99-100
Wallenstein, James, 68
Walla Walla (Washington), prison reform, 125
Walnut Street Jail (Pennsylvania), 45, 47, 94, 108
Ward, Benjamin, 65
wardens, 87, 91, 96
Washington State Prison, 101, 125
wer-geld, 24
Western Penitentiary (Pennsylvania), 48
Whiskey insurrection, 68
white collar crime, 71, 73
white offenders, 76, 77
women's prisons, 61, 104; homosexuality, 105
work, inmates' (see prison, industry)
work release, 91, 123-124, 128-131, 144
workhouse, 29

youthful offenders (see juveniles)

49690

365
C   Clark, Phyllis
         Elperin

Doing time

DATE			
OCT 16 '81			
NOV 3, '81			

Springfield High School
Learning Materials Center